A LIFE UNDER RUSSIAN SERFDOM

Regions of the European part of the Russian Empire, c 1800

A LIFE
UNDER RUSSIAN SERFDOM

THE MEMOIRS
OF SAVVA DMITRIEVICH PURLEVSKII
1800–1868

Translated and edited by

BORIS B. GORSHKOV

CENTRAL EUROPEAN UNIVERSITY PRESS
BUDAPEST NEW YORK

©2005 by Boris B. Gorshkov

Published in 2005 by

Central European University Press
An imprint of the Central European University Share Company
Nádor utca 11, H-1051 Budapest, Hungary
Tel: +36-1-327-3138 or 327-3000 – *Fax:* +36-1-327-3183
E-mail: ceupress@ceu.hu – *Website:* www.ceupress.com

400 West 59th Street, New York NY 10019, USA
Tel: +1-212-547-6932 – *Fax:* +1-212-548-4607
E-mail: mgreenwald@sorosny.org

Translated by Boris B. Gorshkov

ISBN 978 963 7326 15 8 paperback

Library of Congress Cataloging-in-Publication Data
Purlevskii, Savva Dmitrievich, 1800–1868.
A life under Russian serfdom: memoirs of Savva Dmitrievich Purlevskii,
1800–1868 / translated and edited by Boris B. Gorshkov.
    p. cm.
Includes bibliographical references and index.
ISBN 9639241997 (hardbound) – ISBN 9637326154 (pbk.)
1. Purlevskii, Savva Dmitrievich, 1800–1868. 2. Serfs–Russia--Biography.
3. Serfdom-Russia-History-19th century. 4. Russia–Rural conditions.
I. Gorshkov, Boris B. II. Title.
HT807.P87 2005
306.3'65'092–dc22
                              2004027453

Printed in the USA

CONTENTS

LIST OF ILLUSTRATIONS

NOTES ON THE TRANSLATION

This translation is directed at the general reader as well as at scholars and students of Russian history, peasant studies, or serfdom. Wherever possible the translation provides bibliographic notes, references, and suggested further reading on the events, individual persons, places, and things mentioned in the memoirs. Reference notes contain basic facts regarding events, places, or people in order to help the general reader with the historical setting The further reading suggested in the references will help students and scholars with additional historical investigation.

The translation assumes that most readers do not read Russian. In most instances I have therefore used the English equivalents for Russian terms, which follow immediately in parentheses. In most cases I have used the standard Library of Congress method for the transliteration of the Russian spellings of Russian given names, patronymics (middle names), and surnames. Customarily, in Russia people have three names: the given (first) name, the middle name (patronymic), and the surname (family name). For example, the autobiographer's full name is Savva Dmitrievich Purlevskii. The Russian middle name (patronymic) is derived from the father's given name. Along with the person's given name, the patronymic is used as a polite or formal form of address. In his memoir, Purlevskii often uses patronymics. In a few cases, the memoirist wrote only first initials when he wanted to conceal a person's full name. In these instances, where it was possible to identify the mentioned individuals, I have provided their full names in the notes. The names of certain historical figures, such as Catherine the Great, are given in an anglicized spelling form. Names of cities, places, and rivers are given in a manner familiar to those who read English.

Direct transliteration is used for the titles of Russian-language publications in those notes that contain suggested further reading. I am assuming that the further reading suggestions will be taken up mostly by specialists in Russian, studies who are familiar with Russian. For those with no knowledge of Russian, I have provided titles of a few English-language studies.

Throughout his memoir Purlevskii uses many specific expressions, idioms, and slang, peculiar to a Russian commoner living during the first half of the nineteenth century. My principal task was to preserve the original meaning. Therefore, whenever possible, I have used direct translations. Otherwise I have sought American or English equivalents, providing a note with the original Russian version for those who read Russian.

All dates are given in the Russian (pre-1917) calendar of the period, which was used in the original text. This calendar was thirteen days behind the Western and modern Russian calendar.

INTRODUCTION

Savva Dmitrievich Purlevskii, a former serf from Yaroslavl' province, wrote his memoirs shortly before his death in 1868. The literary and political journal *Russkii vestnik* (Russian messenger) published them in 1877.[1] Their publication epitomized the intellectual interest in the life of common people during the late nineteenth and early twentieth centuries. In this era several serf memoirs appeared in Russian literary journals or were published as books.[2] But Purlevskii's memoirs stand somewhat apart. Unlike most ex-serf memoirists, such as the famous Aleksander Vasil'evich Nikitenko who gained freedom from serfdom at the age of eighteen and became a distinguished statesman and academician, Purlevskii

---

[1] "Vospominaniia krepostnago, 1800–1868," *Russkii vestnik: Zhurnal literaturnyi i politicheskii* 130 (July 1877), 321–47, and ibid. 130 (September 1877), 34–67.

[2] During this time the Russian literary journal *Russkaia starina* (Russian antiquity) published a series of ex-serf memoirs; among them were the diaries of A. V. Nikitenko, recently translated with a fine introduction by Peter Kolchin. See Aleksandr Nikitenko, *Up from Serfdom: My Childhood and Youth in Russia, 1804–1824*, transl., Helen Saltz Jakobson, intro. by Peter Kolchin (New Haven and London: Yale University Press, 2001). Others were "Istoriia moei zhizni i moikh stranstvii: Rasskaz byvshago krepostnago krest'ianina N. N. Shipova, 1802–1862," *Russkaia starina* 30 (1881); "Vospominaniia krepostnago," *Russkii arkhiv* 6 (1898); and M. E. Vasilieva, "Zapiski krepostnoi," *Russkaia starina* 145 (1911). Vasilieva's memoirs are also available in English: see "Notes of a Serf Woman," transl. John MacKay, *Slavery and Abolition* 22 (April 2000).

never rose to social eminence. He never occupied prominent positions in the government, nor achieved high professional status. For the most part he lived within the peasant and petty bourgeois environment. In his late forties, some twenty years after he had escaped from servitude, he became a merchant and sales manager (*kommercheskii agent*) of a sugar corporation. This was the extent of his accomplishments. This makes Purlevskii's memoirs unique and brings his personal experiences in servitude closer to those endured by many millions of Russian serfs.

Savva Dmitrievich Purlevskii was born a serf in 1800 in Velikoe, a serf village in Yaroslavl' province of central Russia. In 1831, at the age of thirty, Purlevskii escaped from serfdom by fleeing to the south, beyond the Danube river, where he joined the Nekrasovtsy, an Old Believer group. His first thirty years, therefore, he spent in servitude. In his memoirs, Purlevskii tells the story about both his life under serfdom and his experiences in his childhood and youth. He includes recollections about his parents and grandparents and about his family in general. He describes family and communal life in his village. He also comments on the peasants' economic and social activities and their interactions with local and state officials. Rich in detail, Purlevskii's narrative provides a valuable snapshot of Russian serfdom at work, its day-to-day functioning and practice. Much of this story is about his personal perceptions of serfdom and life under it.

A few words about Russian serfdom may help the reader to situate Purlevskii's story in its proper historical context.[3] In general, serfdom was a system of tangled relations between the landlords who possessed the land and the peasants who populated and worked it. These relations were characterized by a multiplicity of legal, economic, social, socio-psychological, cultural, and political realms, the sum of which made Russian serfdom the remarkably complex societal institution it was. In its fullness, the institution endured for more than two centuries.

---

[3] Unless otherwise indicated, general conceptions in this introduction are drawn from Boris B. Gorshkov, "Serfdom: Eastern Europe," in *Encyclopedia of European Social History*, 6 vols., ed. Peter N. Stearns (New York: Charles Scribner's Sons, 2001), 2:379–388.

Russian serfdom emerged during the sixteenth century, just when similar forms of servitude had begun to decline in many parts of Western Europe. During earlier centuries, Russian peasants had lived on the land in settlements called communes. The majority of these communes were located on lands belonging either to the state, the church, or individual landlords. Landlords' lands hosted approximately half of the existing peasant communes. Although before the late sixteenth century peasants worked the landlords' fields or paid them a fee for the land they utilized, they, at the same time, enjoyed considerable freedom of movement and in general could live as they wished. In turn, landlords provided the peasants with certain legal protection and general physical security.

The process of "enserfment," that is, the step-by-step economic and legal binding of the peasants to the land and to the landlord, resulted from the conjuncture of multiple historical factors both inside and outside Russia. Well-known external and internal economic, social, and political developments all played a role. Among these were the expansion of states and their centralization, the sixteenth-century revolution in prices, the rapid expansion of markets, the growth of cities, warfare, epidemics, and so forth.[4] The early modern Russian aristocracy perceived the bondage of the peasantry as the best way to meet the challenges of the period, and pressured the state to respond to its needs. From the late sixteenth century on, a series of edicts seriously restricted the peasants' territorial mobility and subjugated them to the landlords' authority. The 1649 Law Code (*Ulozhenie*) definitively fixed millions of peasants on the land, forbidding them to leave their place of residence without proper authorization. During the seventeenth and eighteenth centuries, serfdom matured and approached its apogee and by the early nineteenth century began a gradual decline. The famous 1861 imperial proclamation finally ended the legal bondage of peasants.[5]

---

[4] On early modern European society and economy, see Carlo M. Cipola, *Before the Industrial Revolution: European Society and Economy, 1000-1700* (London: Methuen & Co. Ltd., 1976).

[5] See note 2 in the preface.

One obvious but nonetheless noteworthy circumstance of Russian serfdom was that it existed in a society where peasants outnumbered all other social segments. The peasants constituted approximately 80 to 85 percent of the population, whereas the landowning nobility made up only about 1 percent. Around half of Russian peasants populated lands owned by individual landlords and thus were serfs, the very category to which Purlevskii belonged.[6] Much of the balance of the peasantry inhabited state lands, making up the category of state peasants, a semi-bound category which, by the mid-1800s, outnumbered the serfs.[7] An average noble estate accommodated several hundred serfs, with individual holdings running from several dozens to tens of thousands of people. A few noble magnates possessed hundreds of thousands. With a few exceptions serfs and landlords shared common ethnic, cultural, and religious origins.

Being the overwhelming majority of the population, the peasants were in several senses the essential social group in Russia. For instance, they were the primary source for economy and culture. In the absence of a significant middle class, the peasants' activities

---

[6] In 1795–96, some four or five years before Purlevskii was born, the Fifth Imperial Census recorded 57 percent (9,789,676) of the male population as serfs. In 1835, a few years after Purlevskii escaped serfdom, about 37 percent (10,872,229) of the male population was identified as serfs. Before 1861, according to the Tenth Census (1857), serfs constituted about 49 percent (10,694,445) of peasants and 34 percent of the empire's population. These figures are taken from I. I. Ignatovich, *Krest'ianskoe dvizhenie v Rossii v pervoi chetverti XIX veka* (Moscow: Izd. sotsial'no-ekonomicheskoi literatury, 1963), 16, and V. A. Fedorov, *Pomeshchich'i krest'iane tsentral'nogo promyshlennogo raiona Rossii kontsa XVIII pervoi poloviny XIX veka* (Moscow: Izd. Moskovskogo universiteta, 1974), 3. For a general discussion of these and other categories of peasants, see Jerome Blum, *Lord and Peasant in Russia from the Ninth to the Nineteenth Century* (Princeton: Princeton University Press, 1971), and David Moon, *The Russian Peasantry, 1600–1930: The World the Peasants Made* (London and New York: Addison Wesley Longman, 1999).

[7] A small number of peasants were occupied on church and royal lands, and a few peasants lived on their own lands.

predominated in the Russian economy.[8] Their economic, cultural, and social significance enabled peasants, and specifically serfs, to achieve and maintain a balance between the diverse and often opposing interests of the state, the landlords, and themselves. The economic importance of the serfs simultaneously induced the state to regulate lord–peasant relations and permitted peasants to establish limits on the landlords' and local officials' prerogatives. The simple fact was that the Russian state economy could not function without a certain degree of more or less free peasant and serf activity.

This perhaps helps explain certain legal ambiguities of Russian serfdom, a significant aspect of the institution well worthy of mention. The legislation that established serfdom simultaneously empowered peasants to attain their rudimentary economic and social needs. The very law that attached serfs to the land at one and the same time enabled them to seek temporary employment outside the village, as well as to engage in various trade, commercial, and entrepreneurial activities both within and away from the ascribed place of residence. For example, the above-mentioned 1649 Law Code simultaneously granted serfs the right to leave the village temporarily in order to seek employment or to pursue other economic activities. By the end of the eighteenth century, about a quarter of the peasants (including serfs) of the central Russian provinces temporary migrated each year.[9]

On the one hand, landlords sometimes bought, sold, and punished serfs at their whim; on the other, the state banned the sale and mortgage of serfs without land, outlawed advertisements for such bargains, and protected serfs against "unreasonable" corporal

[8] The serfs' entrepreneurial and commercial activities receive attention in Alfred J. Rieber, *Merchants and Entrepreneurs in Imperial Russia* (Chapel Hill: University of North Carolina Press, 1982), and William Blackwell, *The Beginnings of Russian Industrialization, 1800-1860* (Princeton: Princeton University Press, 1968). For Russian-language studies, see Fedorov, *Pomeshchich'i krest'iane*.

[9] Boris B. Gorshkov, "Serfs on the Move: Peasant Seasonal Migration in Pre-Reform Russia, 1800-61," *Kritika* 1 (Fall 2000), 632, 636.

punishment. In any case, Russian serfs were usually bought and sold with the land they populated, a legally sanctioned transaction which signified the transfer of estates or parts of estates to new landlords. During the late eighteenth century, a few landlords were tried for causing the death of their peasants, deprived of their noble status, and sentenced to hard labor in Siberia for life.[10] During the first half of the nineteenth century, over a hundred noble estates were under state guardianship because of the landlords' mistreatment of serfs. In these cases the law limited the authority of landlords over the estates and serfs. Also worthy of note is the fact that, notwithstanding the initial legal prohibitions on complaining against their landlords, in some cases serfs sued the lords in state courts and succeeded in bringing to trial those who overstepped their rights.[11]

Despite its fundamental purpose of preserving hierarchy, serfdom simultaneously opened the door to a certain societal mobility for serfs. It is important to emphasize that neither the state nor the

---

[10] *Istoriia krest'ianstva Rossii s drevneishikh vremen do 1917g.* 3 vols., I. V. Buganov and I. D. Koval'chenko, editors-in-chief. Volume 3, *Krest'ianstvo perioda pozdnego feodalizma, seredina XVII v - 1861g.* (Moscow: Nauka, 1993), 273.

[11] Although serfs' denunciations of their landlords were generally prohibited, the law permitted serfs to complain against their landlords in cases when peasants suspected treason or activities against the emperor, and in cases regarding census (*revizii*) falsifications. In certain cases serfs could seek legal protection or freedom from serfdom in courts and state institutions. *Svod zakonov Rossiiskoi Imperii. Zakony o sostoianiiakh* (St. Petersburg: Tip. Vtorago Otd. Sobstvennoi E. I. V. Kantseliarii, 1842), nos. 952, 1038, and 1039. It is not clear, however, how the state reinforced the restrictions on serfs' complaints. Studies show that serfs complained against their lords on most occasions when they believed that the landlords had mistreated them or deprived them of their interests. Many landlords were sued and sanctioned for the abuse of their serfs. For further discussion of serfs' complaints, see Elise Kimmerling Wirtschafter, *Social Identity in Imperial Russia* (DeKalb: Northern Illinois University Press, 1997), 118-120, and Peter Kolchin, *Unfree Labor: American Slavery and Russian Serfdom* (Cambridge, Mass.: Belknap Press of Harvard University Press, 1987), 142-148.

landlord had an interest in completely binding the peasant. In order to sustain the national economy and the economic needs of the landlords, the state needed to provide the peasantry, Russia's predominant social group, with certain legal protection and freedom for territorial mobility and economic and social pursuits. All these institutional and legal factors underlay the internal dynamics, developments, and changes in serfdom that Purlevskii describes in his story.

In addition to the legal restraints on the landlords' authority, Russian serfs possessed a broad range of extralegal means to curtail the lords' influence. Serfs created and maintained traditions, customs, values, and institutions that provided for their survival by keeping a balance between external forces and their own individual and communal interests and needs. The family and commune were two such institutions. Purlevskii devoted many pages of his memoir to his family and the village commune to which he belonged.

Most Russian serfs lived a meaningful part of their lives in extended, usually two-generational families, although nuclear households were not uncommon among serfs in northern Russia.[12] The structural complexity of serf households often mirrored a particular stage of family development when a young couple lived with their parents (and even grandparents) under the same roof until they gained enough wealth to separate and start their own households. The state and common law recognized the right of every nuclear couple to establish its own household.

Peasant marriages were performed according to local traditions and also enjoyed full legal and customary sanction. A couple's parents would negotiate the marriage contract, as illustrated by Purlevskii when he recalls his own marriage, the arrangements for which were carried out by his mother. He married at the age of eighteen, which, in his own words, "was nothing unusual" (part X) since the average marriage age of serfs was lower than that of nonserf peasants. According to an anthropological study, the marriage

---

[12] Peasant family structure in the northern provinces is analyzed in E. N. Baklanova, *Krest'ianskii dvor i obshchina na russkom severe, konets XVII - nachalo XVIII v.* (Moscow: Nauka, 1976).

age of male serfs in the central Russian provinces ranged from eighteen to twenty-five and of female serfs from seventeen to twenty-one, whereas in the southern regions the average marriage age for serfs was even lower.[13] Landlords did not usually intervene in marriage contracts and did not separate serf families. In some cases serfs paid the landlord a certain marriage fee that differed from place to place.[14]

Regarding family affairs and strategies, as well as actual decision making, the family enjoyed a significant degree of autonomy from the landlord. Grandfathers, known as patriarchs, usually headed the family and had the first say in making decisions about family affairs and daily activities. Even so, important family issues involving the household economy, property, inheritance, and the marriage of children were commonly the subject of meetings of all adult family members. Decisions on such major issues reflected discussion and compromise. Patriarchs represented the family in all communal and estate institutions.[15]

Serf families lived in villages, which were settlements with household and communal buildings, a church, and a cemetery, all of which constituted the peasant commune. The commune was perhaps the most important economic, juridical, social, and cultural institution of the serfs and of all peasants. It had a broad range of functions and responsibilities in village life. The commune

[13] T. A. Bernshtam, *Molodezh v obriadovoi zhizni Russkoi obshchiny, XIX-nachala XX v.* (Leningrad: Nauka, 1988), 43–46.

[14] A 1722 law prohibited landlords from intervening in the marriages of their serfs or from forcing serfs to marry against their wishes. *Svod Zakonov*, 180, no. 949. On the topic of serf marriages see John Bushnell, "Did Serf Owners Control Serf Marriage? Orlov Serfs and their Neighbors, 1773–1861," *Slavic Review* 52 (1993): 419–45; Peter Czap, "Marriage and the Peasant Joint Family in the Era of Serfdom," in David Ransel, ed., *The Family in Imperial Russia* (Urbana, Ill.: University of Illinois Press, 1978): 103–123; and Steven Hoch, *Serfdom and Social Control in Russia: Petrovskoe, a Village in Tambov* (Chicago: University of Chicago Press, 1986), 93–95, 103–118.

[15] M. M. Gromyko, *Mir russkoi derevni* (Moscow: Molodaia gvardiia, 1991), 167–176.

was the setting for interactions between the landlord, the state, and the serfs. The communal meetings consisted of all family heads and through them were managed the village economy and resources, fiscal issues, as well as various social and cultural affairs. The communes consulted the landlords about financial and labor duties, taxes, various obligations, and military recruitment. The commune authorities redistributed obligations and duties among the households, controlled the redistribution of land and resources, and managed the village economy (whether agricultural, cottage industrial, or commercial). It also made decisions about communal festivals and holidays, often supervised the moral behavior of villagers, and resolved intra- and inter-village conflicts. The commune authorities filed suits in the courts and represented the serfs' communal interests in state and juridical institutions. In this capacity it sought adjudication and protection when serfs had been deprived of their rights by their landlords or by anyone else.[16] Purlevskii described many of these communal activities in his own village commune. In the late 1820s, when Purlevskii was serving as a bailiff, his village commune founded a school for the village serf children and built several other communal buildings. The landlord funded the building of the village school.

In addition to its important economic, social, and juridical functions, the commune, indeed village life as a whole, fostered a collective consciousness among serfs. Through village life—rich in tradition, customs, local celebrations, and holidays—serfs maintained a sense of solidarity and cohesiveness. Solidarity among serfs often helped peasants to launch popular protests when the quality of justice deteriorated. The village commune was a principal element in initiating and carrying out popular protest. Purlevskii describes several outbreaks of popular protest on neighboring estates. He also portrays the ability of the peasants to oppose the landlords' oppression and restore justice. Throughout Russia

---

[16] On peasant communes see Jerome Blum, "The Internal Structure and Polity of the European Village Community from the Fifteenth to the Nineteenth Century," *Journal of Modern History* 43 (December 1971): 541–576, and idem, *Lord and Peasant.*

serfs most often protested against rises in manorial dues and service demands upon them on the part of the landlords. Between 1800 and 1861, about 50 percent of the 793 peasant riots and disturbances in central Russia, the location of Purlevskii's village, reflected increases in manorial obligations.[17]

Although Purlevskii frequently complains about his landlord's attempts to increase rent, his village, in his own words, does not seem to have been exceptionally burdened with manorial obligations in comparison to other estates described in his story. On average, Russian serfs paid between 30 and 50 percent of their annual income in rent. However, this payment could range between 17 and 86 percent, depending on the area and on the economic conditions of individual serf families. In areas where agriculture was the leading part of the economy, serfs performed labor duties (corvée, known in Russian as *barshchina*), working roughly half of their time (usually three days a week) for the landlord and the rest for themselves.[18] In areas where agriculture was combined with non-agricultural pursuits, peasants paid rent. Rent and corvée were the two principal instruments of the serfs' economic exploitation by the landlords. Serfs who paid rent in money enjoyed a greater degree of autonomy from the landlords, a factor that aided these serfs in their own independent economic pursuits.

Although often overlooked, regional and local differences in serfdom cannot be overemphasized. Russian serfdom was by no means monolithic. It differed from region to region, and even from one individual estate to another. The nation's diverse geography, climate, and ecology, not to mention widely differing local conditions and arrangements, lent serfdom a very strong regional and local character, which in turn heavily influenced the serfs' economic status and their occupational identities. Although, in general, agriculture prevailed throughout Russia, the extent of the non-agricultural economy, especially in Russian central provinces, was

---

[17] Fedorov, *Krest'ianskoe dvizhenie*, 48–50.

[18] The 1797 law limited serfs' labor duties to three days a week and prohibited work on Sundays. *Svod zakonov*, 184, no. 965.

quite high.[19] The area's geography and climate stimulated the development of various cottage industries and crafts, which in turn promoted trade and commerce. Studies of the peasant economy in the central provinces suggest that between 65 and 90 percent of the region's peasant population was engaged, at least part-time, in one or another non-agricultural pursuit.[20] In certain villages of the area, such as in Velikoe, Purlevskii's native village, non-agricultural economic pursuits completely predominated. Although everywhere in Russia serfs were normally multi-occupational, those who engaged exclusively in non-agricultural activities were not a rarity. The theme of the serfs' independent economic and social activities pervades Purlevskii's narrative. His story, therefore, provides a good illustration of economic and home life in a non-agricultural village, a matter that has until now drawn too little attention. Purlevskii's insights are also valid, however, for all serf villages to the extent that their occupants pursued independent economic, cultural, and social activities.

A brief description of Yaroslavl' province's geography and economy will help the reader situate Purlevskii's story. The province lies in the eastern part of Russia's central-industrial region, so called for its traditional non-agricultural economic orientation. At the time, the area had vast forests divided by large navigable rivers (Volga,

[19] This area was known as the Central Industrial Region. It included the provinces of Yaroslavl', Kaluga, Kostroma, Moscow, Nizhnii Novgorod, Tver, and Vladimir. In 1857 serfs constituted the majority (about 55 percent) of the region's male population and 20.3 percent of the male serf population of Russia. Fedorov, *Krest'ianskoe dvizhenie*, 19.

[20] For a discussion of peasants' proto-industrial activities see Richard L. Rudolph, "Agricultural Structure and Proto-industrialization in Russia: Economic Development with Unfree Labor," *Journal of Economic History* 45 (March 1985): 47–69; Rieber, *Merchants and Entrepreneurs*; Blackwell, *The Beginnings*; Arcadius Kahan, *The Plow, the Hammer and the Knout: An Economic History of Eighteenth-Century Russia.* (Chicago: University of Chicago Press, 1985); and Blum, *Lord and Peasant in Russia.* The figures are taken from N. M. Druzhinin, *Gosudarstvennye krestiane i reforma P. D. Kiseleva* 2 vols. (Moscow: Izd. Akademii nauk SSSR, 1946–58) 2:296–390 and Fedorov, *Pomeshchich'i krest'iane*, chapter 3.

Sheksna, Mologa, Unzha and Vetluga). The area's poor soil fertility and scarce arable lands hampered its agriculture but simultaneously encouraged the development of various crafts, trades, and commerce. A description of Yaroslavl' province dating from 1794 pointed out that agriculture hardly provided the local peasants with an adequate annual subsistence. The majority of the province's population already spent most of its time on various non-agricultural activities.[21] By the mid-eighteenth century, most serfs of Yaroslavl' province paid rent in kind or in money, which also stimulated their interest in non-agricultural trades and in commerce. According to some estimates, by 1858, about 88 percent of Yaroslavl' province serfs paid money rent.[22]

During the first half of the nineteenth century, agriculture lost further ground to local industry and commerce. The province had established broad commercial ties with the port of Archangelsk, the low Volga cities, and Russia's imperial capitals of Moscow and St. Petersburg. In the entire province, only the Rostov district remained primarily agricultural. Non-agricultural trades were particularly well developed in the south-western districts of the province, closely connected to the Volga and therefore to Moscow and St. Petersburg. Yaroslavl' peasants engaged in a broad array of handicraft, trades, and non-agricultural labor activities including seasonal labor migration, (called *otkhozhie promysly*), river faring, shipbuilding, the production of linen cloth and sheepskin coats, oil production, leather-tanning, and horse-breeding. By far the oldest and most characteristic of local pursuits was the production of linen cloth. In the mid-nineteenth century, the province produced for sale about 10.65 million meters (15 million *arshin)* of linen fabrics.[23]

The village of Velikoe, located in Yaroslavl' province, was known

[21] Fedorov, *Pomeshchich'ikrest'iane*, 116.

[22] V. A. Fedorov, *Krest'ianskoe dvizhenie v tsentral'noi Rossii, 1800–1860* (Moscow: Izd. Moskovskogo universiteta, 1980), 33.

[23] G. S. Isaev, *Pol' tekstil'noi promyshlennosti v genezise i razvitii kapitalizma v Rossii, 1760–1860* (Leningrad: Nauka, 1970), 70.

as the center of the province's linen production.[24] Velikoe was first mentioned in primary sources in the sixteenth century as an outpost on the commercial land route between the cities of Yaroslavl' and Suzdal'. Local historians date the origins of the village to the beginning of the thirteenth century. At the time of this memoir, the village belonged to the Iakovlevs, one of Russia's big mining entrepreneurial families. In 1780 the Iakovlevs bought the village from I. I. Matveev for 250 thousand rubles[25], an episode mentioned by Purlevskii. The village traditionally had scarce arable lands and paid dues in rent. According to the agrarian historian I. D. Koval'chenko, agriculture produced only 6.2 percent of the annual income of the village residents, while the balance was derived from non-agricultural pursuits. The local serfs carried on large-scale trade in flax, yarn, cloth, and canvas.[26] By the end of the eighteenth century, Velikoe initiated trade in other products and set up businesses, including metalsmith's and blacksmith's works, dyeing, and icon painting. The last, however, did not become a significant local trade. In around 1800, the serfs adopted spinning wheels, which dramatically increased linen production. During the 1820s, when Purlevskii was the estate bailiff, the village developed secondary industries producing tools and equipment for the linen industry, such as reeds and wooden looms. This proto-industrial development continued during the 1830s and 1840.[27]

According to the Iakovlev family's estate records, in 1835, four years after Purlevskii fled the estate, the village had 559 houses and 1,494 "male souls." Of the 559 families, 490 (87 percent) were engaged in a trade or commercial activity. In 1835 the village had 105 shops and stores. In the 1830s there were about 400 looms in the

---

[24] Today the village has become a town (*poselok gorodskogo tipa*) known as Velikoe, with a population of about 5,000, and is part of the Gavrolov-Yamskoi district of Yaroslavl' province. Velikoe produces clothing and shoes and has a community college and schools of veterinary medicine and law.

[25] Fedorov, *Pomeshchich'i krest'iane*, 119.

[26] I. D. Koval'chenko, *Russkoe krepostnoe krest'ianstvo v pervoi polovine XIX veka* (Moscow: Izd. Mosovskogo universiteta, 1967), 240–244.

[27] Fedorov, *Pomeshchich'i krest'iane*, 120.

village, which annually produced 117 thousand yards of cloth valued at 50 thousand silver rubles. Spinning and weaving in Velikoe took place in small manufacturing establishments called "attics" (*svetelki*), where two or three families joined together for work.[28]

Textile production became increasingly the realm of the women, which added to the women's burdens and household duties. According to Purlevskii, during the winter his mother spun fine yarn and in the summer wove cloth and kerchiefs, all of which were destined to be sold at the market (part IV). Their engagement in productive labor provided serf women with cash which they could keep for themselves or spend independently on clothes and luxury items.

The village organized annual exhibitions and set up fairs for the display and sale of locally produced linen cloth. In addition, Velikoe serfs sold a large quantity of linen at weekly bazaars. In 1829, at the village fair, the peasants sold goods of all kinds valued at 348 thousand silver rubles (an impressive sum at that time), including linen cloth valued at 280 thousand rubles. Much of the village's flax and cloth was exported abroad through the port of Arkhangelsk. Velikoe serfs, and Savva Purlevskii among them, were intermediaries in this trade. During the 1850s the peasants of Velikoe and surrounding villages sold flax valued at between 400 and 450 thousand silver rubles, a veritable fortune for this one product alone.[29]

By the mid-nineteenth century the village of Velikoe had become famous, astonishing contemporary Russian and foreign travelers with its crafts and fine linen cloth and canvas. Travelers noted the village's non-agricultural appearance. According to August Haxthausen, a well-known German traveler to Russia, who visited the area in the early 1840s, Velikoe seemed like "a little town" with its open marketplace and houses built in "a new fashion."[30] By the mid-nineteenth century, a good half of the houses had been built of

---

[28] Ibid., 121.

[29] Ibid., 119–120.

[30] A. Gaksgauzen [August Haxthausen], *Issledovanie vnutrenikh otnoshenii narodnoi zhizni i v osobennosti sel'skikh uchrezhdenii v Rossii* (Moscow, 1870) 1:73.

stone. The village marketplace had various shops with many crafts and services.[31] Another prominent mid-century traveler, I. S. Aksakov, commented that the village lacked "any rural features" and "astonished by its wealth." Velikoe's fine linen even won an award at London's famous International Exhibition at the Crystal Palace in 1851.[32] Purlevskii's memoirs, which begin with a description of his grandfather, who, in the late eighteenth century, became the estate bailiff and as such helped launch Velikoe's economic future, serves as an introduction to the village's and region's colorful and by no means over-familiar history (part III).

But how typical was Velikoe's experience for Russia? For the central provinces, where agriculture was poorly developed, this was in fact a common experience. During the first half of the nineteenth century, dozens of former serf and state peasant villages throughout the region transformed themselves into towns, many of which eventually attained official town status. Perhaps the most famous and frequently cited is Ivanovo-Voznesensk, a textile city in Vladimir province, where several eighteenth-century serf traders established textile mills. Over time the former village became a bustling textile city, "a Russian Manchester" in the words of Frederick Engels. In 1871 Ivanovo was granted a city charter.

Ivanovo's example, however, should not obscure the experience of numerous other villages with similar stories. Kostroma, Tver', Vladimir, Yaroslavl' and other central provinces encompassed over a hundred large proto-industrial and commercial villages. Shuia, Kokhma, Lezhnevo, Nizhnii Landekhh, Voshchazhnikovo, and Bol'shoe all made their mark as centers of textile manufacturing; Mstera, Palekh, and Kholui were known as centers of grain commerce, icon painting, and shoemaking. Vorsna and Pavlovo became important regional centers for metallurgy.[33] These proto-industrial

---

[31] Fedorov, *Pomeshchich'i krest'iane*, 121; Isaev, 67, 70.

[32] Fedorov, *Pomeshchich'i krest'iane*, 121.

[33] Ibid., 121–122, 135; Isaev, 70. The topic of Russian proto-industrial villages is explored in Ia. E. Vodarskii, *Promyshlennye Seleniia tsentral'noi Rosii v period genezisa i razvitia kapitalizma* (Moscow: Nauka, 1972). English-language studies on this issue are limited. For a general introduction to Russian

villages, according to contemporaries, surpassed many district capitals in terms of number of inhabitants and the extent of their economic development. They also served as foundations for central Russia's new cities during the second half of the nineteenth and early twentieth centuries. The transformation of these villages into towns and then, in some cases, into veritable cities, underlay much of Russia's urban development.

Another theme of Purlevskii's narrative that deserves attention is the territorial mobility that the serfs so actively exercised. In contrast to many scholarly portrayals, it appears from these memoirs and from other sources that many serfs of this village were constantly on the move. Even as a serf, in his early life Purlevskii himself seemed to spend the majority of his time conducting his business outside his native village and stayed at home only on rare occasions. Recent research suggests a notable nationwide mobility of Russian serfs, both permanent and seasonal, that impressed many contemporary travelers.[34] The extent of seasonal migration among serfs depended on their economic needs and on the regional and local setting.[35] The peasants of Russia's central provinces obviously exercised greater mobility than serfs from the southern agricultural provinces. About 25 percent of the central

---

proto-industrialization see Edgar Melton, "Proto-Industrialization, Serf Agriculture, and Agrarian Social Structure: Two Estates in Nineteenth-Century Russia," *Past and Present* 115 (1987): 69–106; Rudolph, "Agricultural Structure"; Rieber, *Merchants and Entrepreneurs*; and Blackwell, *The Beginnings*.

[34] For a short bibliography on the permanent and seasonal migration of peasants see Gorshkov, "Serfs on the Move." See also David Moon, "Peasant Migration, the Abolition of Serfdom, and the Internal Passport System in the Russian Empire, c. 1800–1914," in David Eltis, ed., *Coerced and Free Migration: Global Perspectives* (Stanford: Stanford University Press, 2002), 324–57. Peasant seasonal migration in Yaroslavl' province receives specific attention in L. B. Genkin, "Nezemledel'cheskii otkhod Yaroslavskoi i Kostromskoi gubernii v pervoi polovine XIX veka," *Uchenye zapiski Yaroslavskogo gosudarstvennogo pedagogicheskogo instituta*. Vypusk IX (Yaroslavl, 1947), 103–105.

[35] For data on migrations in various provinces from 1800 to 1861 see Gorshkov, "Serfs on the Move," 632, and Fedorov, *Pomeshchich'i krest'iane*, appendix.

provinces' male peasants were seasonal migrants in any given year. In 1856, for example, 51,977 (19 percent) of Yaroslavl's 274,700 male serf peasants received travel documents for temporary migration, which often extended far beyond the given year.

The legislation of 1649, which, as mentioned above, completed peasant enserfment, also provided peasants with the possibility of seasonal migration, an opportunity widely utilized by peasants. Later, in order to regulate peasant movement and reduce unsanctioned migration, the state introduced various travel documents, passports, and travel tickets that enabled peasants to stay away from the village as long as they needed. Some lived in cities for as long as fifteen years. Serfs usually acquired their travel documents from bailiffs, or sometimes directly from landlords for a fee. The laws specified the juridical status of peasant migrants. If they lived in cities, they were considered to be "temporary urban dwellers" with virtually complete freedom of economic activity. It should be noted that serf migrants acted within, and in accordance with, the normal network of state laws and institutions.[36]

As mentioned, Purlevskii's story provides a remarkable illustration of how serfdom functioned in a non-agricultural village in a province with a mixed economy. Yet this autobiography also sheds light on why serfdom had declined by the mid-nineteenth century. Most Soviet scholars of serfdom have offered an economic explanation for the decline of serfdom. These historians have traditionally emphasized the "crisis of feudalism" which, they believe, accelerated during the first half of the nineteenth century. In this interpretation, the new "capitalist forms of production" conflicted with the outmoded feudal system and caused peasant resistance. According to this theory, these developments were the major and fatal features that eroded serfdom and finally brought it to an end. Most Soviet scholars have argued that by the 1850s serfdom had become an obstacle to the rapid economic modernization of Russia.

In contrast, the most recent studies question the existence of a general economic "crisis" during serfdom. They suggest serfdom's

[36] Gorshkov, "Serfs on the Move," 634–35.

flexibility and viability and its startling capacity to stimulate and accommodate economic development. The pioneering scholar of this tendency is the British historian David Moon. In a 1996 article, and in later works, Moon suggested and developed the argument that "Russian serfdom was a viable and enduring institution that met important needs of all the sections of Russian society involved because it was characterized more by coincidence of interests and compromise...than conflict and crisis."[37] Purlevskii's story, and in particular the part which describes the peasant economy, illuminates the latter approach. It describes the peasants' profound abilities to exercise various economic and social pursuits with relative freedom from the landlords. This is a story of how the serfs, often portrayed in history as "backward" and "isolated," proved capable of transforming their "traditional" villages into "modern" urban, industrial areas, as testified to many mid-nineteenth-century travelers.

Purlevskii's story nonetheless reveals a crisis, although not an economic one. This crisis signified a deepening cultural conflict between old and new social perceptions and values, a crisis between growing expectations and the abilities of people to achieve these expectations under serfdom. Despite serfdom's capacity to facilitate economic development and accommodate many of the serfs' needs, serfdom became increasingly viewed as a social and moral evil. The dominant language of the period, clearly reflected in Purlevskii's and other writings, denounced serfdom's oppressions and humiliations.[38] People could no longer come to terms

---

[37] David Moon, "Reassessing Russian Serfdom," *European History Quarterly* 26:4 (1996), 515; idem, *The Russian Peasantry*; and idem, *The Abolition of Serfdom in Russia, 1762-1907* (London: Longman, 2001). For recent treatment of the issue see Roger Bartlett, "Serfdom and State Power in Imperial Russia," *European History Quarterly* 33 (2003): 29-64.

[38] Popular views of serfdom are analyzed in Boris B. Gorshkov, "Democratizing Habermas: Peasant Public Sphere in Pre-reform Russia," *Russian History* 32 (Spring 2005): 5-17; for Russian-language studies see V. A. Fedorov, "Trebovania krest'ianskogo dvizhenia v nachale revoliutsionnoi situatsii, do 19 fevralia 1861 g.," in *Revoliutsionnaia situatsia v Rossii v 1959-1861 gg.*, M. V. Nechkina, editor-in-chief (Moscow: Izd. Akadenii nauk SSSR, 1960), 133-147, and idem, *Krest'ianskoe dvizhenie.*

with the very idea of serfdom or its existence. Relative economic freedom aside, Purlevskii views serfdom as a harsh bondage, a condition unjust and unacceptable to humankind. Numerous Russian-language studies illustrate that such critical perceptions of serfdom, already widespread among peasants, were greatly magnified before the emancipation. Nor was this attitude limited to the peasantry: most of the enlightened Russian intelligentsia, members of the nobility, and government officials held a negative view of serfdom as well. Even Tsar Nicholas I, usually portrayed as an arch-conservative, called serfdom an "unmitigated evil."

The language of freedom and equality prevailed in Russian society not only among the educated elites who read the Enlightenment philosophers; it also penetrated the minds and discourses of the common folk, most of whom were hardly familiar with Enlightenment literature. One may suggest that the views held by the serfs reflected their everyday experiences and interactions. Purlevskii's narrative illustrates the author's personal perceptions but it also reflects the general peasant mood with respect to serfdom. As a literate person who was interested in reading, Purlevskii may have read some of the Enlightenment philosophies. But his discussion of freedom and equality is always concrete. He understands freedom not primarily as the ability to pursue one or another occupation but as liberation from serfdom. He conceives equality as being like people of the "free" social estates. Purlevskii identifies all social grievances and economic problems with the existence of serfdom. One may go so far as to say that for him serfdom is a scapegoat for everything that went wrong. His belief in natural freedom and equality, and his desire to "free [himself] from bondage," rather than the quest for economic opportunities (part XVI), influenced Purlevskii's decision to escape serfdom in 1831.

Serfdom continued to prove its economic and social viability. In the eyes of most nineteenth-century Russians, however, it had become a culturally outmoded and morally unacceptable institution. The new cultural perceptions reflected in Purlevskii's memoirs finally brought it to an end in 1861.

THE MEMOIRS
OF SAVVA DMITRIEVICH PURLEVSKII
1800–1868

PREFACE

This is the autobiography of a serf who came from an initially prosperous but then impoverished family. It tells the story of a peasant who knew sorrow in his youth, who fled beyond the Danube, and who, because of the All-Merciful Manifesto,[39] returned to end his life in Moscow as a guild merchant. In this capacity he was the agent of a large enterprise, a person known in all stock exchange and commercial circles and respected by all. This is an authentic chronicle, written by the author in the twilight of his life. Although many former serfs became outstanding for one or another reason, there is probably no other example of a person who, having just escaped serfdom, remained close to the peasant and petty bourgeois environment and wrote his own memoirs. For this reason alone the pages that follow are worthy of our attention. Alongside the historical significance and curious details of the memoir, of general interest are the author's independent attitudes about the "lords" and the peasant brotherhood, as well as the gentleness and sense of his judgments.

Unfortunately, the manuscript could not be printed in its original form, firstly because it comprises an apparently unfinished

[39] The 1861 edict issued by Tsar Alexander II abolished serfdom in Russia by freeing millions of landlords' peasants. The edict marked a new era in Russian history known as the period of great reforms. For further discussion of the abolition of serfdom, see David Moon, *The Abolition of Serfdom*; and *Emancipation of the Russian Serfs*, Terrence Emmons, ed. (New York: International Thompson Publishing, 1970).

draft, and secondly because it abounds in repetitions and is at times unnecessarily wordy, something that is quite natural for intelligent and literate but poorly educated people. It was therefore necessary to clarify the text in order to make it simpler and more accessible, as the author himself would have done had he had greater writing skills. However, while editing the text and omitting repetitions, I added hardly a single word of my own and tried to preserve the author's unique style.

The original manuscript (112 large-format pages covered in small handwriting) was presented to me by a close Moscow acquaintance of mine, I. D. Gv., a great friend of the deceased author, who, just before his death, placed the manuscript at Gv.'s disposal.

N. Shcherban
Editor of *Russkii vestnik*

1.
Meeting of a peasant commune

2.
Blessing of a betrothal of a peasant couple

OUR VILLAGE,
ITS INHABITANTS AND OWNERS

(I)

Our birthplace, the village of Velikoe ("Great"), Yaroslavl' province (thirty-five versts[40] from Yaroslavl' city eastward along the main road to Rostov), had, from time immemorial, along with the surrounding villages, belonged to the sovereign's court department. A church, two market days a week, and the production of peasant shoes, mittens, gloves, and woolen stockings remain relics of those old days. Traditionally, these crafts sustained the local market, which in the summer was enlivened with the additional sale of cloth and fine handkerchiefs (perhaps even better known than the village itself), and, during the winter, became brisk with the sale of a type of flax called "glinets." The area historically produced a large quantity of flax, which was always famous for its quality. In the eighteenth century the entire estate, with all its twenty-three hamlets and the village of Pleshcheevo, somehow (I cannot explain how, probably Ekaterina gifted it[41]) passed into the possession of Prince Peter Ivanovich Repnin.[42] This dignitary loved the village,

---

[40] *Versta* is a pre-revolutionary Russian measure of distance. One *versta* is approximately 1.067 km or 0.663 mile. Thirty-five *versts* is about twenty-three miles.

[41] Here Purlevskii is referring to Empress Catherine I (r. 1725–1727). Her reign is explored in John Alexander, "Catherine I, Her Court and Courtiers," in *Peter the Great and the West: New Perspectives*, Lindsey Hughes, ed. (Basingstoke, UK: Pargrave, 2000), and Lindsey Hughes, *Russia in the Age of Peter the Great* (New Haven: Yale University Press, 1998).

[42] Here the author apparently means Prince Anikita Ivanovich Repnin

built a wooden mansion there where he frequently lived himself, befriended the contemporary governor, maintained a kennel with hounds of a special breed, hunted rabbits with his guests, and went out searching for bears. He was so fond of home building, adding, and rebuilding that his whimsical refurbishments kept the peasants busy with lots of work. In return he did not greatly encumber the peasants with money obligations and gave them freedom in every-thing else. The elderly people even used to brag: "What a life it was under the prince! Local zemstvo[43] officials never showed up. When we happened to get drunk and got up to mischief, we would get away with it: we would go in the morning to express our regrets to the prince, take a little treat for the butler, and no one would be any the wiser. If any bold spirit stepped forward to complain against us and make claims, he would be treated with a whip in the stable."

The prince definitely protected his peasants and did not burden them with rent. But it was bad that he did not care about the estate economy at all and, in this respect, he did not serve as a good ex-ample to his peasants. His kindness turned into an indulgence of evil. People became villains, they drank and were lazy and did not bother to learn how to make money. At that time, the village had only two stone peasant houses, although both were very signifi-cant—one of them because its owner, a serf, made bricks himself,

---

(1668-1726), a military commander and politician during the reign of Peter I. Anikita Repnin led the Russian army at the Battle of Poltava (June 1709). For his military achievements Repnin was given the Order of An-drei Pervozvannyi and granted Velikoe. On the reign of Peter the Great see Paul Bushkovich, *Peter the Great: The Struggle for Power, 1671-1725* (Cambridge, UK: Cambridge University Press, 2001); M. S. Anderson, *Peter the Great* (London: Longman, 1995); and Hughes, *Russia in the Age of Peter*. For a discussion of the Battle of Poltava see Robert Frost, *The North-ern Wars: War, State and Society in Northern Europe, 1558-1721* (New York: Longman, 2000). On Repnin see V. I. Buganov and A. V. Buganov, *Polkovodtsy XVIII v.* (Moscow: Patriot, 1992), 187-198.

[43] *Zemstvos* were the local governmental bodies, which should not be confused with the local representative government *zemstvos* established after 1864.

and the other for another reason. The owner of this house was a tanner of raw leather. Once, when an epidemic occurred among the cattle, he skinned the deceased animals, cured the hides under the prince's protection, and sold them for a big profit. Thus, with the help of carrion he built his mansion. People say that, besides the brick-maker, perhaps only one other person earned his bread by fair work: the elderly man who bred doves and for several years took them to Moscow on the order of a well-known notable who lived there at that time. (The breed is still famous.)

The neglected economy of the village soon made itself apparent. Affluent peasants were practically absent. Eventually, the prince suddenly found himself in need of money. First of all, he appealed to his own peasants, offering them freedom with all their land and forests for a redemption fee of sixty thousand for 2,500 souls, which meant twenty-four rubles a soul. The peasants could not muster even that! When they had duties to pay, if the prince did not help, they would often get into trouble.

What came of this story of the prince's need for money? Of course, the estate was sold. In those days people were sold easily, like cattle. If the landlord happened to need money, several peasants would be taken to the market. Any free person could buy serfs—no formal deed of purchase was needed, only a written landlord's acknowledgment. An entire estate could be turned over to the marketplace. There were special people for this, something like dealers (these dealers were also solicitors in courts and had friendships with affluent people). With the help of such a dealer, our entire estate was sold to a rich man from the merchant class (*kuptsy*[44]), not to a nobleman.[45] The merchant, Savva Iakovlevich

---

[44] *Kuptsy* (pl.), *kupets* (sing.), was a social estate in Russia and usually referred to the upper-middle-class people who engaged in large-scale commerce or business. On the topic of Russia's middle classes, see Rieber, *Merchants and Entrepreneurs*; Blackwell, *The Beginnings*; and *Entrepreneurship in Imperial Russia and the Soviet Union*, Gregory Gurov and Fred V. Garstensen, eds. (Princeton: Princeton University Press, 1983). Russia's middle classes also receive attention in Elise Kimmerling Wirtschafter, *Social Identity*, chapter 3.

[45] According to other contemporary sources, the village was sold to

Sobakin (he later changed his surname to Iakovlev),[46] was an alcohol tax farmer.[47] Elderly people said that this Savva Iakovlevich originally came from the Ostashkovo *meshchane*,[48] that he worked in St. Petersburg for a court supplier of vegetables, and that he was a handsome man, blooming with health—a man of excellent appearance. He knew how to present himself to people and was in high favor with certain persons of that time who knew how to make a landless peasant (*bobyl'*) into a rich man. I am not sure whether it was luck or ability and natural wit that brought Savva Iakovlevich into the good graces of so many influential nobles. But one day, on a special occasion, free drinks were served in all St. Petersburg's drinking establishments, as a sort of treat for the people. Relying on his patrons, the tax farmer charged the treasury far more money than he had really spent—the sum was twice as much or more than his entire annual income. This time he had gone too far, but, more importantly, he had fallen out with someone. A de-

---

Savva Iakovlevich Sobakin (Iakovlev) in 1780 for 250 thousand rubles by I. I. Matveev, who was apparently a local real estate dealer. Fedorov, *Pomeshchich'i Krest'iane*, 119.

[46] The Russian surname Sobakin is derived from the word *sobaka* (dog). This name was probably considered to have an unfortunate ring to it, which might have caused its owner to change it.

[47] The imperial Russian state possessed a monopoly on alcohol (and some other goods, including salt) and sold the right to retail trade in these commodities in tax farms to merchants (or sometimes nobles), who paid a fixed amount to the state and retained the rest of the income as a profit. In 1863 the state eliminated alcohol tax farming. On this issue see John LeDonne, "Indirect Taxes in Catherine's Russia: Liquor Monopoly," *Jarbucher fur Geschichte Osteuropas*, 24 (1976): 175–207; R. E. F. Smith and David Christian, *Bread and Salt: A Social and Economic History of Food and Drink in Russia* (Cambridge, UK and New York: Cambridge University Press, 1984); and David Christian, *'Living Water': Vodka and Russian Society on the Eve of Emancipation* (Oxford, UK: Clarendon Press, 1990). For Russian-language studies see V. V. Pokhlebkin, *Istoriia Vodki*, 2nd edition (Novosibirsk: Russkaia Beseda, 1994).

[48] The *meshchane* was a social estate in Russia and referred to the urban petite bourgeoisie (townspeople). *Ostashkovskie meshchane* were townspeople from the city of Ostashkovo, in Tver' province.

nunciation was issued—Savva Iakovlevich lost his tax farm and was himself expelled from St. Petersburg.

Of course this was unpleasant, but with money one can live well anywhere. He therefore bought our princely estate, as well as Demidov's metalworks in Siberia and a linen manufacturing establishment in Yaroslavl', with one thousand hereditary serf workers.[49] As for St. Petersburg and Moscow, he owned many houses in both places.

Whether before that time or after, I do not know, he had five sons and a daughter: Peter, Ivan, Gavrilo, Mikhail and Sergei. Customarily, sons of affluent people could enter state service, receive a rank, and eventually enter the nobility.[50] After the death of their father, the five sons (all unmarried) divided the estate into five parts. Sergei, at the time already a lieutenant-colonel, got our village without the surrounding hamlets, 3,051 acres (1,130 *desiatinas*[51]) of arable land, 432 acres (160 *desiatinas*) of forest, 1,620 acres (600 *desiatinas*) of meadowland, and, in addition, he inherited the Siberian metalworks with souls attached.

From the time the rich tax farmer bought the estate, peasant life took on a different form. Unbound freedom turned into slavish obedience; reproaches were heard from all sides regarding the

---

[49] Savva (Sobakin) Iakovlev later became one of the biggest metallurgy entrepreneurs in Russia. He owned several large metalworks in Siberia and the Urals, including the famous Alapaevsk mill. For more information on Iakovlev's enterprise see *Metallurgicheskie zavody na territorii SSSR s XVII veka do 1917*, M. A. Pavlov, editor-in-chief, 2 vols. (Moscow: Nauka, 1930) 1: 17, 107, 175, 195, 380.

[50] According to various state provisions, among the different ways of achieving noble status was promotion to rank eight in the civil service or to rank fourteen in the military. Affluent non-nobles of the free estates could enter either civil or military service. For further discussion of this issue see Paul Dukes, *Catherine the Great and the Russian Nobility* (London: Cambridge University Press, 1967); idem, *Making of Russian Absolutism, 1613-1801* (New York: Longman, 1982), and Brenda Meehan-Waters, *Autocracy and Aristocracy: The Russian Service Elite of 1730* (New Brunswick, NJ: Rutgers University Press, 1982).

[51] *Desiatina* is a pre-revolutionary Russian unit of area. One *desiatina* equaled 2.7 acres.

peasants' past deeds; rural bureaucrats began to visit the village endlessly, with or without reason, and practically lived and ate there; now there was no longer any princely protection—now everything had to be paid off with money! The new owner set up a cotton mill on the river near the village and forced everyone who could not pay the designated rent to work there—in other words, almost the entire estate. Only then did the senior people realize that in order to get rid of the heavy corvée one needed to seek a means of making money. But in contrast to the old days, people went too far to the other extreme. Everyone began to care only about himself, resorting to any small-minded calculations and any means to get money. Then, realizing their past miscalculations, the elderly men began to say, "God is angry with us—our life has been made dismal because of our sins." Others would add, "God is against us not for our impudent behavior under the prince but because we ceased to believe in the Old Scriptures; we've been ruined by the Nikonshchina[52] and life with tobacco users." Homegrown intellectuals even began to speak about the last days, about the seal of the Antichrist, and about the imminent appearance of the beast with the title 666. However, the contemporary priests not only paid no attention to the state of peoples' minds but themselves further demoralized the peasants by their own way of life. These ignorant rumors reinforced the schism among all who revered the

---

[52] The Nikonshchina refers to the reforms within the Russian Orthodox Church introduced by Patriarch Nikon (r. 1652-1658). These reforms aimed at making religious scriptures and liturgies used by the church uniform and clear from textual corruptions. The reform stirred up opposition and provoked a schism within the church. Those who opposed Nikon's ideas became known as the Old Believers. On this topic see Robert O. Crummney, *The Old Believers and the World of Antichrist: The Vyg Community and the Russian State, 1694-1855* (Madison, Wisc.: University of Wisconsin Press, 1970); Nicholas Lupinin, *Religious Revolt in the Eighteenth Century: The Schism of the Russian Church* (Princeton, NJ: Kingston Press, 1984); Paul Meyendorff, *Russia, Ritual, and Reform: The Liturgical Reforms of Nikon in the Seventeenth Century* (Crestwood, NY: St. Vladimir's Press, 1991); and Roy R. Robson, *Old Believers in Modern Russia* (DeKalb, Ill.: Northern Illinois University Press, 1995).

importance of Christian ceremonies. Speculations about crossing with two fingers and performing church services according to the old texts preoccupied all weak minds, and especially women.[53] They fell victim to Pokhomych, who was one of the major teachers of the schism (although, on the sly, he was fond of the bottle). He established a chapel in the village.

Although I am not sure about the specific years when all these things happened, I know that our predecessors lived in this disastrous corvée state for about fifteen years until the division of the estate, mentioned above, among the heirs of the rich tax farmer. It must have happened well before 1800, because in 1790 the young owner, the lieutenant-colonel, declared, by written order, that the peasants of our village (1,250 souls) were liberated from factory work and that they owned all the arable and meadowlands and forest for an annual rent of fifteen thousand paper rubles. The annual state revenue dues were 1.5 rubles a soul. For that time this landlord's rent seemed quite burdensome; besides that, the peasants got less than 2.7 acres (one *desiatina*) per soul of arable land— only enough for grazing cattle; as for planting grain, don't even bother thinking about it! Our elderly people were almost in tears thinking of the time when the prince had asked only sixty thousand for the entire estate and it would have been free for ever, but they had not been able to collect the money because of their dissipated life at that time.

There was nothing that could be done—the past cannot be brought back! People began to say, "Thank God we at least got rid of the corvée. Although the rent is heavy, it is still better for the peasants to make a penny. Women can be of help here: they are good at weaving fine new articles that visiting merchants praise and pay a lot of money for. Also, we must be grateful to the young lord for allowing us to elect a bailiff ourselves. Someone from our own village, whoever he is, is still better than a stranger. Take for

[53] Purlevskii's attitude toward women reflected the universal male view. For a discussion of this, see *Becoming Visible: Women in European History*, Renate Bridenthal et al., ed. (Boston: Houghton Mifflin Company, 1987).

example the mill manager, a stout German. However well one accomplished one's work, if one did not bring the manager a treat for a holiday—eggs, butter, or towels and cloth—one would get into trouble. The damned manager would carp at anything and order a flogging. And there was no one to complain to. If the manager could not find anything to pick on, he would ask you to enter his room, and if you accidentally got dirt on the floor, he would get you to lick it off or to wipe it with your beard, and the unpleasant man would not let you go unless you wiped it clean..."

In my youth, these stories told by the elderly people made little impression on me. When I remembered them later, they reinforced my belief that our peasant dependence was bitter!

(II)

Although not an unkind man, our new owner, the lieutenant-colonel, was, right from his childhood, undisciplined. He had no particular interest in the sizable circle of his father's family friends and even felt it burdensome to make visits. He lived independently. As a result, the old ties with his family friends were destroyed and even his relatives did not want to keep contact with him. In their place he found other people, anxious to please—unattractive individuals, fond of drinking, going on a spree, or meeting a beautiful face, willing to praise his virtues and his wisdom of Solomon, and loving gossip. His life went on smoothly. A table for thirty or more people of various rank and gender was laid copiously every day. At six the dinner came to a close, the windows on Nevskii[54] were shuttered (the lieutenant-colonel lived in St. Petersburg), and the fun began: musicians, singers, and a buffet. Before drinking, they usually cried, "Brothers, fill the wineglasses and drain them to the bottom!" Then there would be singing and dancing. When they got tired of this they would put soft rugs in the hall, sit on them, and

---

[54] Nevskii Prospekt is the main street in St. Petersburg.

strike up with their beloved "Down the Mother Volga River."[55] When this too got tiresome, another game awaited: dressing in their Adam's suits in a warm room...[56]

Those who wanted not only to take advantage of the booze but to play cards in the rich gentleman's house also wormed their way into our lord's favor. The ring-leaders of this "golden cut company," as they were called—people subtle and shrewd—conducted their business skillfully. They lured along several young nobles who loved to gamble. Although he himself was not particularly fond of gambling, the landlord, enticed by the kindness of his notorious visitors, would sometimes participate in the games and lose. What was it to him to lose several thousand rubles! Once he gained a fat profit from the sale of iron to a foreign company. His fellows sniffed it out. They came to lunch, carrying with them a sack of gold coins (*chervontsy*).[57] Others appeared when the lieutenant-colonel, already full and drunk, holding a glass of wine, uttered his usual verse, "Well, friends, God gave us wine for our pleasure. In it, old age will find youth and all misfortunes shall be over." They joined in, drank well, and then started gambling. The money was laid out on tables. Initially they placed small bets, so that even the lord himself, not a great gambler, became disappointed to see that nobody wanted to stake more. In order to encourage the game he himself placed bets at all tables: three won, one lost. Overall he won about ten thousand rubles—not a big gain for a rich person. The lord just wished to encourage his guests, and soon left the gamblers for diversion in another room.

"Sergei Savich!" the guests cried, "The game has again become boring without you."

"Well," he said, "I'll show them now!"

---

[55] "Down the Mother Volga River" (*Vniz po matushke Volge*) is a Russian folk song known among the popular as well as elite classes. It was specifically popular among barge haulers.

[56] The idiomatic expression "in Adam's suit" probably meant without clothing and the "warm room" would have been a sauna or steam room.

[57] *Chervonets* were golden coins of five- and ten-ruble denomination in pre-1917 Russia.

He came in, looked for the table with the largest pile of money on it, and took six cards—"I bet everything!"

He lost...

There was nothing to do but pay. "How much?" he asked. They counted the heap of gold coins and calculated its value at two hundred thousand in banknotes... He ordered the steward to pay the money in full and got himself roaring drunk that evening.

Besides his bragging and his habit of going on sprees, our lord also adored horses, about which he possessed no sense but wanted to outdo everyone else. This sort of horse lover is a big find for horse dealers. They rounded him up—befriending his servants and coachmen. At first they dealt honestly with him, but then began to palm off every kind of jade on him. These purchases packed the lord's stables, both in the city and in the country. When the horse dealers realized that the lord had no more space for horses, they began to use different tactics. They would come to him, and one of the more persuasive among them would start:

"Ah, little father, Sergei Savich, your horses are just great but they have become restless and you keep them stabled all the time. You had better get some fresh ones. There are some steeds coming from Bitiug, of the Mosolov breed, which are just right for you. Here is a certificate!"

"Well fellows, as to purchasing I would certainly do so, but I have no more room. Perhaps we could do an exchange?" he replied.

"If you please, father—anything, if only to please your Excellency..."

The lord ordered an exchange of three horses, plus some cash in addition, for one horse; otherwise the horse dealer would never have left him alone.

That was how our domestic affairs went. The steward, Ivan Savich Skvoznik, a shrewd person, enjoyed the unquestioned confidence of our lord. During his ten years of service for the lieutenant-colonel, the steward studied him well, accommodated himself to all the lord's whims, and gained control of everything. He was incredibly accurate in maintaining records. Whenever the landlord wanted to check his finances, everything would seem to be in place, to the last penny. Only it did not occur to him that with every sale of iron and copper, with every purchase for the estate's needs, Ivan Savich gained a huge profit, paid to him by the merchants and suppliers in order to get him to sell for less and buy for more. He made a fortune. When it happened that the lord was short of cash— whether the iron had not yet been sold off or the rent not yet received—and he needed some for his daily expenses, the lord would say, "Take care of this, dear Savich. Find money wherever you can and pay what has to be paid." Savich would then use his own money but pretend that he had borrowed it for a paid-in-advance Jew's interest.[58] He pretended to be a poor man, and to prove his poverty and keep the lord's favor he married one of our serf lasses—not unknown to the lord, so people said, who then gave her freedom and two hundred rubles. The money, of course, was a matter of indifference to Skvoznik but the woman was handy. She took care of the household as a housekeeper—it was convenient to work together.

There was also a fellow, the chef, some *mus'e* (monsieur). He was in charge of purchasing provisions and wines, in a word—for the buffet, the lord's table and the servants' meals—but in reality he in fact did almost nothing. He would come every morning to the lord, wearing a white jacket and a cap, and made a bow. Then he would drop into the kitchen to give the cooks the order for the day's menu and afterwards walk to a fellow-countryman's wine shop for a drink and a snack. And then he would visit his suppliers with his own interests in mind. By lunchtime the chef would return, check the kitchen, have his lunch at a special table, and after that go to the wine shop again and stay there until midnight, smoking pipe tobacco and sipping Madeira and grog. It was not too bad though, for he kept everything in order. What was bad was that he skimped a lot on the servants' provisions. There were many servants of various ages and genders, over a hundred, and many of them were without even a piece of bread. Servants and cooks could perhaps get something from the lord's table, while the poor

---

[58] In his text Purlevskii wrote "za zhidovskii rost vpered."

musicians and singers frequently bawled and blew on empty bellies.

And we in the village also had hard times. We needed to pay the rent in full and, besides, had to send our best fellows to serve as menials in his house. In one year alone, forty people were taken as musicians, servants and carriage footmen, and then the lord wanted twenty girls.

Finally, this careless, happy-go-lucky life got on the lord's nerves. Suddenly he stopped carousing and displayed an interest in theater. He rented a box at the theater and went there almost every evening. As table companions at his huge dinners there remained only those who also loved theater. The house calmed down, the junkets stopped, and the gambling company lost its warm shelter. The lord even became concerned about cleanliness, changed his garments every morning, dressed foppishly, and made visits somewhere... Suddenly, he gave orders to refurbish the countryside house and buy new furniture for it. And he left for the country house earlier than usual. People began saying that the lord was going to marry some actress.

And so it happened. The house obtained a mistress, Nastas'ia Borisovna, who, the very day after arriving, called together all the household servants and asked them about their work and if they needed anything. She was so kind and nice to them that the servants hardly knew how to appreciate it. Order prevailed. It was suggested to Skvoznik that he look for another job, and the chef was also dismissed. They set up a home office to maintain the household records, put the main cash-desk in the lord's study, and in place of the steward hired a butler from among our own serfs, a kind, good man. From that time on everyone in the house was well fed and happy. Favorable rumors about the lord's new life spread around the city and reached his brothers. Their former coolness gradually began to disappear. At first infrequently, as if informally, the lord's former friends started to visit him as well. And the lord, along with his young spouse, also became a frequent visitor at gentry houses. So everything went well.

The family happiness lasted for nine years. In those years life was good for everybody. The number of household servants decreased by half; some obtained their freedom. The birth of every daughter (God did not provide sons) was reported to the estate administration, and the priests were given a hundred rubles for their service. When the great fire occurred in our village, the peasants were exempt from rent payments for a year and, moreover, were given subsidies for rebuilding. In the tenth year of their marriage, Nastas'ia Borisovna, two weeks after giving birth to her seventh daughter, passed away... She was buried in Lavra[59] under a grim tombstone upon which is carved a little nest with nestlings.

With her decease the daughters came under the supervision of governesses; although the reined-in former uproar was not restored to the house, nor did the established order prevail; visits were thinned out and occurred only if someone came by to see the children. The lord also almost abandoned his own house and frequently stayed in another—whose German mistress, so people said, began to give birth to babies that looked like him, and where food provisions, servants, and the carriage were constantly sent. It was also heard that this German family consequently gained half a million rubles in Treasury Bonds.

And so it went until 1808, when, due to the rupture with England, iron sales there stopped.[60] Steel prices fell dramatically and the estate mills' profits decreased so much that the lord was hardly able to sustain the mills' serfs. Then, suddenly, his elder unmarried brother died. He had been known as a miser, about which one could judge by the fact that he never sold his metal but stocked it instead, so that after his death a pile of iron pressing deep into the ground was found. He saved money as well. One could do nothing with the iron at that time, but since one-quarter of the miser's property went to our lord, his business improved. Consequently, in the year 1812, he was able to make a large charitable donation for which he received the title of state councilor (*statskii sovetnik*). Later on, as the result of another donation, he was granted the rank

---

[59] The cemetery of the Alexander Nevskii Lavra in St. Petersburg.

[60] Purlevskii is referring to the continental system introduced by Napoleon in 1806, which prohibited trade with Britain by closing continental ports to British ships.

of active councilor (*deistvitel'nyi sovetnik*). With the rank of general, the lord was more willing to make visits and himself received visitors. Soon his two grown-up daughters were married to generals.

The lord died in 1817. His heirs were two married ladies and five adult girls, who soon also got married. By mutual agreement, and without the division of the estate, they established a common estate management under the title "The heirs of such and such person."[61]

---

[61] The enterprise came to be known as "The Heirs of S. S. Iakovlev." It also included the metalworks in Siberia and the Urals, a linen mill in the village, and the Bol'shaia Yaroslavskaia Manufactura, a famous linen mill in Yaroslavl'. See *Metallurgicheskie zavody*, and N. Paialin, "Bol'shaia Yaroslavskaia Manufactura v 50–80-kh gogakh XIX veka," in *Istoriia Proletariata SSSR*, A. M. Pankratova, editor-in-chief, 5 vols. (20) (Moscow: Sotsekgiz, 1934): 93–106.

3.
Peasant betrothal

4.
Peasant betrothal

MY GRANDFATHER

As serfs belonging to the same person who paid a set rent and worked only rarely for the lord and who were therefore not over-worked in the estate mills (unlike in earlier times) and living with-out pressures from outside officials, our predecessors possessed full freedom to develop their own economic life. The village's central location, its twice-weekly markets, its two-week fair in Sep-tember, and the villagers' own sharpness all assisted them. They only lacked honesty and integrity. Therefore not many of our peas-ants prospered. Nor was the way of life at that time pleasant. The houses clearly revealed poverty—out of over six hundred houses in the village, only ten were made of stone and no more than ten of the wooden houses were much different from huts by appear-ance.

One of those stone houses belonged to our family, which, from time immemorial, had enjoyed the respect as well as the confi-dence of those even outside the local and town residents. I do not know anything about my family's forebears, except that, in the past, they had lived in one of the estate's twenty-three hamlets, a place called Purlevo. That is why, when they moved to the village under Prince Repnin, they came to be called Purlevskie (from Pur-levo). I heard a lot about my grandfather, Petr Petrovich. My late father, Dmitrii Petrovich, had a great appreciation for his business and often talked about what he himself had witnessed. My clearest memory is when the village commune elected my grandfather bailiff. Having prayed to God, he called the entire commune to the village office and said:

"Orthodox Christians, I have called you in not to make a rent payments redistribution—this should continue as it is now and everyone should pay attention to it himself. My duty now is to look after things so that everything will get better. I must tell you frankly about your disastrous situation, of which you yourselves are the cause. I will speak sincerely of myself as an example for you. My prosperity came from fair and hard work. No one can reproach me for laziness or dishonesty. If we, by Almighty Providence, must be serfs, at the same time we have not been deprived of the means to better our way of life. Although the arable land we have is not enough to sustain ourselves, we have the freedom of choice to do everything we can. The location of our village clearly compensates for the scarcity of arable land, because it provides the means for trade and for other business for everyone and as everyone pleases. We are sometimes clever in domestic trade, but how many of us really make good use of it? Everyone comes to the marketplace, but many of us bustle about the whole day for the sake of a kopeck or two. Nor do we get anywhere with crafts: we work just as in the times of Tsar *Gorokh*[62]. Indeed, we have no good *kalatch*[63] in the village, no spice-cake to treat visitors, and no smithy to shoe a horse. When the villagers from round about have sold their goods at our market, what can they buy from us apart from knitted wear and shoes? They make their purchases from other people! Other people make a more profitable use of our own market than we do."

The villagers replied to my grandfather:

"We don't have anything to start with, poor people that we are..."

Then he changed his tone:

"Listen," he said, "I'll tell you how it is. The cause of our wretched life is not poverty but the absence of accord among us— the schism in our faith, and unfairness and deception among us. That is why we do not trust one another. Were we poor but still

---

[62] Tsar *Gorokh* (peas) is a Russian epic and literary character who lived and reigned in time immemorial. The expression "Like under Tsar Gorokh" usually refers to something old, out of fashion, and outdated.

[63] A kind of fancy Russian loaf.

honest and just people, we would have abilities. Unpleasant talk spreads around about us. Nobody will rely on us, because we cannot rely on ourselves. Let's make a decision that from this day on we will all bail one another out for such and such an amount of money, according to each person's ability and behavior.[64] What bail each one deserves will be decided by specially elected people. They would issue annual guarantees. In case of complaints against someone, we will collect the money he owes, bail him out, and force this person to repay the amount. If someone squanders the loaned money they should be deemed harmful to the commune and sent into tsarist service."[65]

In order to get things started, my grandfather offered two thousand rubles from his own savings for ten years with no interest. The purpose of this was to create a common fund for anyone who needed to borrow money so they could begin trade. In return they would have to pay six kopecks annually for each ruble. Agreement was achieved by consensus. This agreement was written on paper and kept in the commune office. Initially they collected 6,500 rubles in total, which subsequently, because of interest and other fees, increased to 30,000.

From that time (this happened in 1794), our peasants seemed to be reborn and began to look after one another. In no more than three years the formerly empty village square was lined with shops.

[64] Village communes often practised what became known as *krugovaia poruka* (collective responsibility). For a general discussion see David Moon, *The Russian Peasantry*. For Russian-language literature see V. A. Alekandrov, *Sel'skaia obshchina v Rossii (VII - nachalo XIX v.)* (Moscow: Nauka, 1976); idem, *Obychnoe pravo Krepostnoi derevni Rossii, XVIII-nachalo XIX v.* (Moscow: Nauka, 1984); and L. S. Prokof'eva, *Krest'ianskaia obshcina v Rossii vo vtoroi polovine XVIII-pervoi polovine XIX veka* (Leningrad: Nauka, 1981).

[65] His grandfather was probably referring to the tsarist military service. Transgressors of the law were often sent into the army. On the topic of Russian military service before 1861 see Jon L. H. Keep, *Soldiers of the Tsar: Army and Society in Russia, 1462-1874* (Oxford: Clarendon Press, 1985), and Elise Kimerling Wirtschafter, *From Serf to Russian Soldier* (Princeton: Princeton University Press, 1990).

They sold not only small articles but luxury goods and everything that the peasant household needed. Smithies were built. Instead of old-style shoes the village shoemakers began to produce German boots with sharp toes and creaks. Even the neighboring lords bought them with pleasure. The villagers gradually built oil mills and put several brickyards into operation. The sale of flax and linen canvas expanded. The peasants also began to sell their goods at distant markets.

My grandpa remained bailiff from 1794 until 1802 and tried to keep everything in good order. He introduced bookkeeping, for which purpose two young fellows were taught accounting. My grandfather, Petr Petrovich, passed away in October of 1802, at the age of sixty. How did it happen that he was able to make himself into such a personage? This is how. His elder brother lived in Moscow for many years as a merchant's assistant. He brought his younger brother (my grandpa) to Moscow, where he lived for twenty years. He worked first as an errand boy and then as an assistant to a very smart individual from whom my grandpa learned Muscovite trading habits and other things. After his return to the village, he engaged in trade himself. When his son, my father, grew up and became his dependable assistant, my grandfather had the free time to look into the conditions of his fellow villagers, figure out their problems, and think up the means to solve them.

During the winter, grandpa's commerce consisted of purchasing flax and handmade peasant yarn. Some of the former was sold locally to traders traveling from various localities, but the biggest part went to Vologda merchants for the port of Archangelsk. Later he sold flax directly to the Popov Archangelsk trading house. The peasant yarn supplied linen mills in Yaroslavl' and Kostroma for canvas and ticking. In the summer, he bought peasant yarn, as well as narrow peasant linen canvas, both twisted and smooth. Both types were sold to Moscow merchants—the twisted for the Ukrainian market and the smooth for Moscow and for state suppliers. The volume of his trade was quite considerable. Grandpa's finances reached twenty thousand, a great sum in those times!

In family life, my grandpa was well known for his hospitality. Food was always abundant: various kinds of pies and tarts, home-brewed beer and white honey were never lacking. In those days people drank little tea but grandfather already had a tea-set with a copper teapot. The set looked lovely behind the glass of the blue cupboard and was used only for occasions: after a bath or after a long trip in cold weather, or on holidays when the village priest with his wife and our close relatives visited. When city visitors came on business, the copper teapot sat prominently on the table. They would drink a glass of *nalivka*[66] with their company, but nobody in all his life saw grandpa drink. He held himself and everyone at home under strict discipline. My late father was no exception to the rule and got hardly less than all the others. Even after he was married he still tried to hold himself in hand in his father's presence. "Where fear is—there is piety, too," grandpa used to say. And no one grumbled about him. Only much later my mother recollected on occasions that "the breadwinner was strict, and, if he noticed something wrong, he would glance at you in such a manner that would give you a shiver. He was not impolite though." Grandfather was handsome in appearance and eloquent. "At some relaxed moments he would speak in such a charming way that one could listen to him forever," my dad used to say.

Not long before his death my grandpa went to Moscow, prayed in the Kremlin cathedrals, and visited the Trinity Sergius Monastery.[67] He brought back a small samovar from which, it seems, he did not drink. Soon he was overcome by illness. Before he died, grandpa asked for the icon of Our Lady of Kazan', blessed my father, and solemnly said:

"Well, my dear son, from this time on you are the full master of your life. Be a good Christian and son of the Orthodox Church.

---

[66] Home-made fruit liqueur.

[67] The Trinity Sergius Monastery (Troitse-Sergieva Lavra) was founded by Sergius and Stefan in 1342, forty miles northeast of Moscow. Today, the monastery houses a monastic community and remains the center of monasticism of the Russian Orthodox Church. Near the monastery lies the city of Sergiev Posad. For more information about the monastery see Scott M. Kenworthy, "The Revival of Monasticism in Modern Russia: The Trinity-Sergius Lavra, 1825-1921," Ph. D. diss., Brandeis University, Waltham, MA, 2002.

Respect your mother and remember me, love your wife and son, and stand for the truth. All the property goes to you but my holiday suit is for my grandson—let him remember his grandpa. Donate one hundred rubles to the church and give one hundred to the priests for their service. Give my cane and fur hat to Father Semen. This is my last word in the presence of the Invisible God."

These words exactly were written down by my dad, and the letter was given to me by my mother after my father's death. My grandpa died upon taking the Last Communion, saying farewell to the family and in full consciousness. So it was said about his death.

5.
Peasant dinner

6.
Scene of peasant family life

MYSELF, MY CHILDHOOD, AND MY FAMILY

(IV)

At the time when grandpa died, my dad was already about thirty. He had acquired excellent trading skills. With his own money and the confidence he gained from people, he maintained the household with no difficulty. Besides him and my mom, Dar'ia Egorovna, our family included my grandma and me, then aged two. (I was born on 5 January 1800.) I remember myself from the age of four. From that time on my memory retained everything. I knew, and remember well, the appearance of my relatives; I remember the things I enjoyed then and my habits; I remember the troubles I had. I remember how my late father strictly discouraged my pranks. Sometimes he was lenient with me out of respect for my grandma. Only she could obtain mercy for my sins. On occasion my mother would say to her husband, "What a strange habit you have of scaring the child, he is so frightened that he fears everybody." My father's response would be short: "Shut up." With my grandma it was different. She would tell my dad, "Well, Mitia,[68] I endured enough fear when our deceased grandpa disciplined you. Now I won't let you take liberties with this kid. This is the only child we have. If he gets sick and dies..." Father did not contradict her but only smiled and went away.

One of my pranks I will never forget. On the Day of the Advent of the Holy Spirit, my father and mother went to another village for a church service. I was left at home with my grandma. I felt so free

---

[68] A pet name for Dmitrii.

to do what I wanted! All morning I literally did not feel the ground under my feet, as though flying in the air. Then an old idea came into my head. My friends often used to brag when they found something: one found one thing, the other found something else. Sometimes they would show an old half-kopeck coin or a rusty five-kopeck piece dug up from the ground. But I had never happened to find even a quarter-penny: I had nothing to brag about. After I was tired of running around that day, that old idea occurred to me again: there were sacks with copper coins under father's bed, twenty-five rubles in each... I took out one, untied it, and saw that it was filled with stained half-kopeck and five-kopeck coins from Catherine's time. Well, I took a handful, as much as I could take in my hand, trying to grasp as many coins as I could. Near our house there was an empty piece of land where, in the past, there had stood a house of a prosperous childless elderly man. I buried the coins in various places there, marked each place, and then went to my friends. They were playing knuckle-bones.[69] I approached them, said conspiratorially that I had found two five-kopeck coins and one half-kopeck coin hidden in the empty lot, and showed them my discovery. The guys left their knuckle-bones and immediately marched to the place. I followed them, too. One guy would start digging at one place, another at a different one, but all without success. But I found either a half-kopeck or a five-kopeck coin everywhere I dug. I amazed everyone, and even I myself felt an unrestrained excitement. In the meantime, my grandma was sitting on a bench by our house with other peasant women. Several times I brought her my "discoveries," and she and her company started talking about the former owner, the childless elderly man, who in reality did indeed hide his money. Meanwhile, the evening was approaching; my father returned. My grandma began to brag about my good fortune. Dad listened to her in a sort of emotionless, cold way, then he stared at me, and probably at that very moment realized what the truth of the matter was. He ordered the servant to

[69] Knuckle-bones was a popular game among all social classes in Russia.

take care of his horse, while he went to the room and looked under the bed. He pulled out one sack, then the other, and glanced dubiously at the knots. He counted the money and found two rubles missing. I was standing in the next room, neither alive nor dead. Then I heard dad call me. I entered. Father asked strictly:

"That is how you make your discoveries. You are too young to swindle! Tell me, who taught you this?"

The tears sprang from my eyes and I fell on my knees: "Dad, dear! I am guilty. I did it myself. Nobody taught me." And I told my dad how for a long time I had been so disappointed that I had not found anything while my friends had. My grandma and mother watched in silence, waiting for father's reproof. But father, having listened to my confession, addressed only my grandma, "That, mom, is what happens when a child grows up without proper care." Thus, the rod was not used but I was required to make several bows to the ground before an icon.

(V)

I loved my grandmother more than anyone else. But I did not enjoy her support for long. In 1805 she was struck by a serious illness and, after several weeks, passed away. I cried bitterly, apparently not so much because she had died, but mostly because I felt that without her there was nobody to protect me. Although my mother spared me on the quiet, she would not say a word before my father. However, I don't know whether I got more cautious or whether my dad became more indulgent, but I was beaten only on rare occasions, perhaps just when I played knuckle-bones too long and missed lunch. Even then my father would usually look out of the window or come out of the gate and call me, "Saushka!"[70] I would abandon everything, run up to him, and stand as if rooted to the ground: "What do you want, father?" Dad would glance at me and, if everything seemed alright and I had not gotten dirty, he would

---

[70] A pet name for Savva.

say in a serious voice, "It's lunchtime." But if I had gotten dirty, he would pull my hair.

Only once was I punished harshly. I was sitting on a *zavalinka*[71], rocking and quietly repeating a nasty word I had learned somewhere. My father overheard me saying it, sneaked up, and suddenly lashed a belt across my back: "Don't say such words." My mother comforted me with only a drink of water. Why he lashed me, he did not say. I realized that only later.

This is the way I grew up until my seventh birthday. I loved to listen to fairy tales, particularly when Aunt Danil'evna told them. In order to read fairy tales myself, from a book—where, as Danil'evna said, there were many such tales—I began to study reading and writing without saying a word to anyone. I learned some basics and could even combine words, though I hesitated to say anything about it to my father. But he himself noticed that I was always leaning over his books, of which he had many. Once, on one happy occasion, he asked me suddenly, "Maybe you want to study?"

I did not speak.

"Did the cat get your tongue?"[72]

"Yes, daddy," I replied, "I would like to study."

"You are still too young."

However, on the very next trip to Yaroslavl' my father bought me a prayer book and the Psalter. "Well," he said, "now Saun'ka, praise God, the books are ready. Soon you will go to a master." And so it happened. As December approached, on the Day of St. Nahum the Prophet, after the church service, my father himself took me from the church to the parish priest, Ivan Petrovich. They gave me a church edition of the ABC and an ivory pointer. My "master," as we used to call a teacher in our village, in my father's presence, took my hand with the pointer, underlined the first line of letters, and named every letter. I repeated after him, and after that spelled out

---

[71] A small mound of earth or stone around the outer wall of a peasant house.

[72] In the original Russian version: "Cto zhe ty iazyk prikusil?" ("Have you bitten your tongue?"), which means "Why don't you speak?"

myself several times: "az," "buki," and so on, until "zhivete."[73] With that, my first lesson was finished.

It did not require hard work from me to learn the letters and syllable combinations, because I had already seen them at home—although new, the little ABC-book had been my long-time friend. I soon finished learning them both, letters and syllables. But when we approached words under diacritical marks, this did not go well. I completely misunderstood what these marks were for and why. Only with practice did I master this subtlety. I needed to make one more effort: to learn punctuation marks, quotation marks, semicolons, colons and so on. Although, I hardly understood anything, I learned everything by heart. Then we got to the prayer-book and Psalter. I thoroughly memorized all the passages that the teacher assigned and read them carefully. The master, Ivan Petrovich, lay on the top level of the stove[74] and corrected me, though he never paid attention to whether I was reading or speaking from memory. After a year, the reading course came to an end. Then we began to study writing: dashes, curves, then letters, and finally words and sentences themselves, such as, for example, "Who has God, has everything." For about a half a year I scratched and wasted paper...

During all my studies my father never tested me. But once, I remember, on an autumn evening, he asked me to write something. And he took my book of writing samples away from me... I took a pen but hardly knew what to write or how.

"Why don't you write...? " When he saw that I was hesitating, he asked me to write down the following: "In the name of the Father, Son and Holy Spirit."

"I never studied how to write such words," I replied.

"How so, 'never studied'? You have studied how to compose words, so do it."

But I could not do this without the writing samples book: I stared at my pen and did not move.

---

[73] The names of the letters of the pre-1917 Russian alphabet.
[74] Purlevskii is referring to a Russian stove on which people lay for warmth.

I can see it as though it were today. My dad straightened up, looked at me, and said:

"Ah, dear, that's how you've been taught. Well, do you know how to read? Bring the Psalter here."

He opened the book right on the seventh song: "God, Condemn not by Your Anger"—a very appropriate passage, which I knew well. But in the meantime, because of my embarrassment, my memory failed me. I was so confused that I could not put in any syllabic order letters I had learned a long time ago. Then I received a little punishment with a saying: "And you yourself wanted to study." Dad ordered me to become a good reader within three days, otherwise a bigger punishment would await me.

After that day my learning went on by my own effort. Ivan Petrovich, despite the complaints of my father, continued to listen to my reading exercises as he himself lay on the stove. Finally, dad put six rubles in copper coins in a small bag and asked me to hand them to the "master" and give him a bow. However, my education continued at home. My father, although he himself had a limited education, was fond of reading. He did not limit himself to religious books alone. He was interested in contemporary secular literature, too. After his death he left several periodicals, such as *Vestnik Evropy*, *Pochta Dukhov*, and *Zhivopisets*, and among his books, I remember, were works by Karamzin, *Kadm i Garmoniia*, *Zolotoi Osel*, and many other novels and theatrical plays, by the way, by Fonvizin.[75] From money given to me as presents, I also collected my own library. I kept my books on my *polaty*;[76] they included *Eruslan Lazarevich*, *Bova Korolevich*, *Il'ia Muromets* (Ilya Muromets), *Emelia Durachok* (Emelya the Simpleton), *Sem' Simeonov* (The Seven Semyons), and others.[77] My idea of bliss consisted of

---

[75] Denis Fonvizin (1745–92), eighteenth-century Russian author and writer of comedies, author of *Nedorosl'*, translated into English as *The Minor*.

[76] Wooden planking fixed between ceiling and stove, used as a sleeping place.

[77] These books are famous Russian fairy tales. Some are available in English. See *Russian Fairy Tales*, collected by A. N. Afanas'ev, transl. by Norbert Guterman (New York: Pantheon Books, 1945).

reading them during the evenings to the whole family, except for my father. He did not like this practice of mine. Dad did not allow me to read secular literature without his permission. He also assigned me daily readings from *Church History*, *The Lives of the Saints*, and *The Catechism*. He made me explain the meaning of what I had read and rewarded me with a cup of tea. In our conversations he expressed sorrow that he could not teach me the basics of grammar, writing skills, and arithmetic, because he himself had never learned them. In our village, there was no one capable of teaching these things. In the city, serfs were not accepted into schools at that time. Father could only teach me basic accounting and business.

(VI)

Reading under my father's supervision and my conversations with him seem to have facilitated my childhood development and understanding, and I admired him not only as a father but as a knowledgeable person. There was one thing, however, that disappointed me. Unfortunately, my father had a fatal weakness, a strange sort of illness. He normally went a year or more without consuming alcohol. Then, overcome by a kind of illness for two or three weeks running, he would ask only for alcohol and could hardly eat bread. If no one gave him alcohol and no one was paying attention, he would go outside in his underwear and beg everyone he met to give him some wine. Such a respectable person was ready to give up his last possession for a glass of wine! After two weeks of hard drinking he became weak, thin, and overcome with fever. When he tried to get up from the bed, he would fall down in a paroxysm from which it was difficult to awaken him. Everyone at home worried and trembled for his life. His skin peeled in strips from his body and even from his tongue! How did his health endure this?

In truth, my father was sturdily built, clearly a Russian *bogatyr*,[78]

---

[78] A bogatyr is a hero or warrior in Russian folklore.

177.2 centimeters (two *arshins* and eight *vershoks*[79]) tall, not stout but thickset, with light-brown hair, a thick beard of medium length, and large deep-grey eyes. His appearance as a whole reminded one of an old saying of those times: "Be self-confident without haughtiness, and modest without self-abasement." He always dressed in a way appropriate to his peasant status and to his circle: a red shirt worn outside velveteen trousers, a sleeveless cloth jacket and goatskin boots, or a bathrobe. These were the clothes he wore at home. On holidays, during the summer, father wore a dark-blue caftan of fine cloth and a light hat, and in the winter a cloth coat lined with Kalmyk fur and trimmed with beaver, and a golden Persian silk belt. At home he loved order and wanted everything to be clean and neat.

This was the realm of my mother, Dar'ia Egor'evna, a kind and beautiful woman. She did the cooking and maintained the household. In addition, she was a cottage artisan: in the winter she spun fine yarn and in the summer wove canvas and kerchiefs. This meant she had her own money for holiday clothes. In those days, on holiday days, women wore silk *feriazi*[80] trimmed with braid or lace, and a silk jacket. On their heads they wore a pearl-decorated *kokoshnik*[81] covered by a kerchief. At the neck, women wore strings of pearls and a silver cross on a chain. In the winter, the women's clothing consisted of rabbit-fur coats decorated with brocade or damask, kerchiefs, and, if it was very cold, a velvet coat trimmed with marten over the rabbit-fur coat. Women's everyday dress included a white shirt and a red calico *sarafan*[82]. The head was covered with a *povoinik*[83], with a cotton or silk kerchief over it.

Our house was the finest in the village: it was built of stone and had one and a half stories with five large windows on the front side. It had two full rooms and an outer entrance hall, which led

---

[79] Two *arshins* and eight *vershoks* is about five feet eleven inches.
[80] A traditional loose Russian dress without a collar.
[81] A *kokoshnik* was an old Russian headdress worn by peasant women.
[82] A traditional collarless and sleeveless dress.
[83] The *povoinik* was a headdress worn by married Russian peasant women.

into a kitchen with a pantry. The lower level of the house had two storerooms and a closet for goods. One full room served as a living room for receiving guests; the other served as a family sleeping room. We had a male and a female servant. The former lived with us for about thirty years; the female servants sometimes changed, but one woman lived with us for fifteen years.

In addition to his commercial ties, my father enjoyed the favor of local nobles. In particular, the Karnovich family and old Stepan Stepanovich himself were frequent visitors in our house. They were treated with tea and soft pirogi, which my mother was truly skilled at making. In general we ate well: on meat days we would have cold jellied meat, boiled ham, then Russian cabbage or noodle soup, grilled lamb or chicken. We often had goose or duckling. In the fall, young lamb was considered the most delicious dish. The geese, ducklings, and hens were always our own. The foodstuffs we bought were very cheap. Bread was not made from the local harvest but shipped by river from Tambov province. In the spring, on the arrival of the ships, a nine *pud*[84] sack of rye flour cost between six and seven rubles; the same quantity of rye grain between five and six rubles; the best-quality peas eighty kopecks per *chetverik*[85]; the same quantity of the best-quality millet the same price; eight *puds* of buckwheat four rubles; a pound[86] of beef three kopecks; lamb two kopecks; a whole goose thirty kopecks; a duckling fifteen kopecks; a hen even cheaper; eggs four kopecks for ten; whole-milk butter fifteen kopecks a pound; vegetable oil five kopecks a pound; imported salmon, sturgeon, and beluga seven and ten kopecks a pound; red caviar fifteen kopecks; and the best Kazan' honey between six and ten rubles a *pud*. And all these were sold not for

[84] A *pud* [pood] is a pre-1917 Russian measure of weight. One *pud* equaled 16.38 kg or 36.1 pounds. Nine *puds* is 147.42 kg or 325 pounds.

[85] A *chetverik* is a pre-1917 Russian measure used for dry goods. One *chetverik* equaled 26.239 liters or 6.93 gallons.

[86] The pre-1917 Russian pound (*funt*) was a little less than the American pound. One Russian pound equaled 409.5 grams, whereas one American pound is 453.6 grams. Eight Russian pounds equaled 3.3 kg or 7.2 American pounds. In the text the word pound refers to the old Russian measure of weight.

silver but for copper or paper money. Looking at these prices from sixty years ago and comparing them with those of the present time,[87] one might be led to believe that people were better off at that time.

I would certainly reply that they were not. People were needier in those days. The common folk of the northern provinces lived almost entirely on rye bread and gray vegetable soup. *Kalatch* was considered to be a rare treat, and cake a wonderful gift. Everything the peasant household produced—dairy products, beef, lamb, eggs, and so on—was sold out of necessity. People lived on peas, oats, and steamed turnips. Our village was an exception. Trade and crafts brought us money and made us richer than other villages.

[87] The author is referring to the 1860s.

7.
Old peasant woman telling fairy tales

8.
Peasant boys playing knucklebones

AND MY ADULT LIFE BEGAN...

Our commerce continued in an orderly way, as it had before, but not quite as successfully as it had been in my grandfather's time. A shipment of grain sank, some debtors failed to pay, thus our finances decreased considerably. Nevertheless, in spite of all this my father had no real difficulty with his business. He was not embarrassed by his serf status but often felt a certain sadness when he had to obey the landlord's whims. For example, once the landlord summoned my dad to St. Petersburg and kept him there for almost a year solely to demonstrate to his visitors what peasants he had! Still, relations between my father and the landlord were the best. The lord even empowered my dad to administer the estate and represent him in courts and juridical institutions, where the lieutenant-colonel was engaged in some lawsuit with his nephews. This caused our family much trouble and drew my father away from his own business. But, most importantly, the clerks my father dealt with often tempted him into drinking.

In August 1811, after a bout of drinking, my father got very sick. It happened as follows. He went to Moscow to handle some business errands. There, having got used to partying with officials and clerks, he drank a great deal at a big party and then continued to drink alone the following week. Rumors about it reached our village. We sent a relative to Moscow to rescue my father. Apparently, the relative had no experience in dealing with people in such a state as my dad had gotten himself into. He took a coach and carried my father back home, allowing him neither rest nor vodka on the way. My father arrived back home in such a poor condition that he could hardly get off the coach. They said that his blood had clotted, and his system finally failed him. On 4 September my dad died. He was forty-two years old. In his will he left everything to my mother, asked his friends and relatives to take care of me, and made a note to our servant: "Mikhailo, don't abandon my son and be his advisor in commerce."

From that time on the laboring part of my life began. My mom, although a neat and efficient housekeeper, hardly understood anything about commerce, because my late father had kept her out of his business. Unfortunately, the very year he died he had loaned almost all his money to the Vologda merchants, who then incurred considerable losses at the port of Archangelsk. My mother tried to take care of this and made several trips to Vologda herself, but with no great success. She managed to reclaim only about two thousand paper rubles. At that time I was eleven years old and had no practical commercial experience. My advisor Mikhailo was a loyal individual but was also incapable of anything. My mother had no confidence in our abilities. She kept the money and gave us only five hundred rubles so that I could launch myself in business. With so little money the family's commercial activity slowed down. The winter came to an end with no profit. Then the year 1812 approached...[88] Commerce had declined everywhere, but what would happen to ours? In the village of Velikoe, people hardly thought about business and instead prayed to God for their survival. They buried or hid their belongings and prepared to flee. All the males, from ten to sixty years old, armed themselves with pikes to guard the village at night. All essential items became expensive. Our earnings declined and we spent all the money we had previously saved just to buy basic goods. We held barely five hundred rubles in reserve. As for state and manorial dues, we had to pay them on time and in full, always up to one hundred rubles. My mother wept

---

[88] Here Purlevskii refers to the Russian campaign of 1812 during the Napoleonic Wars, known in Russia as the Patriotic War of 1812. On this war see Alan Palmer, *Napoleon in Russia* (London: Simon and Schuster, 1976), and Eugene Tarle, *Napoleon's Invasion of Russia, 1812* (New York: Octagon Books, 1979).

that the money was running out. Even so, with a great effort we managed to keep up, although we felt sad and woeful about our own misfortunes and those of the poor people who were fleeing Moscow with nothing but their lives. We only breathed freely when Napoleon abandoned the capital[89] and God began to punish him for the horrors he had inflicted on us.

Nevertheless, I know scarcely any details of what happened then, because our region is about two hundred *versts* from Moscow.[90] My curiosity about many significant events remained unsatisfied. I remember only that the bodies of the enemies, who were regarded as the servants of hell, were not buried but burned instead.

(VIII)

By the end of the fall things had calmed down and people gradually began to return to Moscow. There they found everything in ashes and faced a complete lack of foodstuffs and everything else necessary to restore their destroyed households. The lack of goods was experienced everywhere. I decided to ask my mother to allow me to go with Mikhailo to Moscow with goods to sell. At first she hesitated, but finally agreed. With two hundred rubles of my own and three hundred on credit I bought boots, stockings, linen for shirts, and various other merchandise for laboring people. Six days later our carriage safely approached Moscow. We stopped at a coaching inn at the Cross area.[91] The next morning customers came and cleaned us out entirely. Having made a great profit we went on to have a look at Moscow. The outskirts where we stopped showed almost no sign of destruction, but when we went further, beyond Sukharevskaia Square inside the city, we saw devastation every-

---

[89] Even after St. Petersburg became Russia's capital, Moscow also retained the name "capital." It was sometimes referred to as "the old capital," while St. Petersburg was known as "the northern capital."

[90] 200 *versts* is about 213 km or about 133 miles.

[91] Here Purlevskii is referring to an area of Moscow.

where. Even the Kitai-Gorod[92] had a sorrowful look: burnt houses, ruins, windows with no glass, and empty shops. But when we saw the damage to the Kremlin, our hearts pounded and our tears flowed. The two previous years, when I had visited Moscow with my late father, I had seen the Kremlin in all its beauty!

That same evening we returned home. My mother was exceptionally happy with our return home and our good fortune. When she counted the money she saw that, after all our expenses, we had earned over two hundred rubles in profit. I, too, was in a state of excitement. But when we told her about what we had seen we all began to sob and we forgot about our gains...

Profit, however, always remains a lure for people. Within a month we set out again for Moscow with the same commodities. But this time we did not commit the sin of earning big profits, because many other traders elsewhere had brought the same goods in abundance. We recovered what we had spent only with great difficulty, and even suffered a small loss. Meanwhile, life and economic activity had begun to return to Moscow. Since there were still only a few residents in the city, rents were very cheap. With a little money one could find a space for a shop. I thought it would be worthwhile setting up a small *sbiten'*[93] shop. This idea came to me and I knew that I had enough money to carry it out. Our Mikhailo was formerly a *sbiten'* maker and made a great drink.

With these ideas in mind I went back to the village. I thought about it over and over again. Mikhailo also supported the idea and said, "With you I will go for it." I decided to tell my mother. It upset her terribly and she shouted that I had gone crazy. She forbade me even to think about such nonsense and insisted that since "your grandfather and dad were in business here, you should be too."

At that time I had a best friend, Nikita. He was a little older than me. We went together to Ivan Petrovich to study, and on holidays

[92] Kitai-Gorod is an old area of Moscow located by the Kremlin and surrounded by a wall. The area was traditionally populated by craftsmen and shopkeepers.

[93] *Sbiten'* was a traditional Russian hot drink made from water, honey and various spices.

Nikita stayed with us to play and read tales. After my mother had refused, I told him about my Muscovite plan. He quickly understood the idea and explained it to his father, who also saw the point. Nikita and his father dashed to Moscow. They hired a *sbiten'* maker in a village along the way and in two weeks opened a store on Makhovaia Street. After a month Nikita's father returned home and thanked me for giving him the idea. A year later, Nikita visited the village and brought bread and cookies. He told me privately that he had earned three thousand rubles. He took his brother back to Moscow (their father had three sons) and put him in charge of the *sbiten'* store, while he opened a grocer's shop. Within ten years these two brothers (by the name of Lebedev) had made a hundred thousand rubles, bought themselves out of serfdom and married, and by the 1830s possessed big capital and two stone houses. When the first cholera epidemic struck Moscow, the entire family was wiped out.[94]

Meanwhile, when I heard the rumors about Nikitushka's wealth, I had scarcely any regrets but was in fact very proud that my idea and advice had brought him a fortune. I was glad to receive letters and sometimes presents from him. As for me, I still lived in Velikoe and traded flax and yarn for small amounts of money, mostly around the local villages. I had no money to buy a horse and therefore used to go on foot to the local markets and fairs. If I bought something, I sold it right there and, if I made a tiny profit, I went back to my village with it. The work was hard and I made scarcely enough money for me and my mother to live on.

Time passed and there seemed to be nothing awaiting me. In the year 1817, my mother began to make hints about marriage. "You are of age," she said, "and I am not healthy; we have a decent house, we can find a rich bride."

---

[94] The first cholera epidemic broke out in Moscow, St. Petersburg and the central Russian provinces in the fall of 1830. According to some incomplete data, 466,000 people were affected by the disease in 1831, of whom 42 percent died. The disease originated in Asia in the early 1820s and first struck the Caucasus and Astrakhan' regions. Ia. I. Linkov, *Ocherki istorii krest'ianskogo dvizheniia v Rossii v 1825-1861 gg.* (Moscow: Gos. uchebno-pedagogicheskoe izd., 1952), 26-27.

I did not want to disappoint my mother with a refusal and only asked her first to let me go on foot to Moscow to pray to the saints and maybe to find something useful. For some reason my mother readily agreed to let me go this time. My thinking, however, was as follows: since Nikita was now rich, he could scarcely refuse to lend me some two or three hundred rubles, if only for a year, in order to start my own business. With this money I would start up some enterprise.

With high hopes I arrived in Moscow, found my friend, and called to see him. Nikita was no longer what he had been. He greeted me, however, invited me to a tavern, treated me to tea after my long trip, and asked me this, that, and the other about my life. I told him, frankly, that "our life is as it has always been. We work hard and get paid very little, almost nothing. If I had in my hands one or two hundred, I could make a pretty penny even in our village, but I have only about half a hundred in turnover. What can one do with that? Earn about three rubles and go thirty-eight versts[95] back home."

Remembering our old days of friendship, I nearly added, "Would you, brother, lend me some money to start up in business?" But I hesitated. I expected that my old friend would himself ask me: "How much do you need?"

But my Nikitushka realized what I had come for and began to explain that, although he had money, he still needed it himself. He had invested most of his wealth in goods and had almost no cash, although he had debts to pay off.

I had scarcely expected such a pretext and restrained myself from further talk. Nikita asked me:

"How long are you staying in Moscow?"

"I'm leaving for home today."

"Right," he said, "food is expensive in Moscow. It is no joke staying here even for a day."

At the same time he took from his side pocket a wallet loaded with paper money, took out a blue five-ruble banknote, and said:

---

[95] 40.5 km or 25.2 miles.

"Take this. It may be useful on your way back. And take a loaf of Moscow bread with you for our teacher, Ivan Petrovich, as well. He is still alive, I suppose?"

I answered "Thanks be to God, he is alive and well," took the bread, but refused to accept the money. "Thank you for your hospitality and treat, now goodbye and take care," I said, and rushed away from the tavern.

I barely remember how I walked across Moscow and how I found myself eighteen *versts* away,[96] in Mytishchi.[97] There I drank water from a well and took a short rest. That night I stopped at the Trinity Sergius Monastery. I slept well. In the morning I prayed to the saints, and on the third day reached home. My mother had not expected me back so soon. Surprised at my early return, she asked:

"Have you really been to Moscow?"

"I have been, Mother. Only this time I did not like Moscow."

My mother did not ask me any more. She was pleased that I had come back.

[96] Eighteen *versts* is 19.08 km or 11.86 miles.
[97] Mytishchi is a town northeast of Moscow.

9.
Peasant boy

MY MARRIAGE, MY LANDLORD, MY TRADE, AND OTHER THINGS

Not long after my return from Moscow, our landlord sent an order to the estate administration, requiring that the rent be collected two years in advance and that the money be deposited in full with the Moscow Council of Trustees (*Moskovskii Opekunskii Sovet*). (He had made a donation for some charitable purpose.) Those who failed to pay in full were to be drafted into the army. The richer peasants were obliged to pay for those who could not find the money, and by doing so these peasants gained freedom for themselves and their families from future conscription.

The lord's order was read at the village assembly. People talked it over and decided to apportion how much money each household had to pay. As bad as peasant life could be, no one wanted to become a soldier and each tried to fulfill his share. My levy was one hundred rubles. I had only seventy rubles in cash and my mother gave me the other thirty. To help me stay in business she also sold her pearl necklace for one hundred and twenty rubles and gave this money to me. This money really helped me. My trade became brisker and I even got outside credit and bought a horse. In the winter I usually traded in flax and yarn. During the summer, I rented an apple orchard with a friend of mine. This also turned out to be a success. In two months we both gained a profit of eight hundred rubles in cash.

But in the meantime the landlord wrote again to the bailiff, ordering him to select four tall men no older than twenty, who would be suitable to stand on the footboard at the back of his carriage, as well as four beautiful eighteen-year-old girls. All these people were to be taken personally to the landlord in St. Petersburg...

As usual, this order was read out at the village gathering. Nobody dared to complain about it. Everyone, however, was saddened, in particular those who had young sons and beautiful daughters. My mother, too, worried about me. She yelled out, "The old sinner. At his age, to engage in such overindulgence! What if they take you into this service because you have no defense? I will not be able to bear it. I will leave the house and follow you to Piter.[98] I'll bow down to him and ask him to let you go in the name of your father, about whom the landlord often boasted before his lickspittles. And if he doesn't take compassion upon you I will scratch out his eyes. Let God and the tsar be my judge! I am a mother!"

I had never seen my mother in such a state. I could not stand it and began to weep myself and to comfort her, saying that "The bailiff is my father's old friend and will not bring any harm to us. He won't send me into the lord's service. There are many other young fellows in our village who are taller than me."

"Well, Saushka," my mother said, "people do not remember friendliness. You may be saved by something else. The bailiff has a niece. I have heard that he wants to marry her to you..."

Meanwhile, the bailiff was deciding with the elders in the estate administration which families were to send their young sons and daughters. People said that I, too, had been named, but the bailiff himself took me off the list. The fathers of the young people who were selected, regardless of how much they tried to butter up the bailiff, were left to shed tears as they parted with their sons and daughters—and in particular the mothers wept for the fate of their beautiful daughters.

Thus, until 1818, my time was spent on everyday matters. Then my mother again began to talk insistently about marriage. She made it clear that I could choose my bride, but suggested that a tie with a good family would serve us well. At that age I still had no inclination for marriage but promised my mother that I would think about a bride and marry.

---

[98] Piter is an abbreviated name for St. Petersburg.

Not long afterwards Petr Ivanovich, our fellow-villager, arrived. For about thirty years he had been the chief convoy manager of the barges that transported iron from the landlord's Siberian mills to St. Petersburg. This had amounted to half a million *puds*[99] of iron hardware annually. In the village, Petr Ivanovich lived with his family for no more than two months a year. He had a reputation as a kind, good-natured, and honest person. His employees loved him like a father. The landlord himself respected him, and in person and in his letters called him nothing but Petr Ivanovich. In the village, too, everyone greeted him with low bows. My late father was a friend of his, and since he had an only daughter it was often said that we "shall become relatives, with God's blessing." I often used to stare at this girl, who was a year younger than me. We played together in the summer, and in the winter went tobogganing. Now, in my present situation, I could hardly hope that her family would agree...

But still I hoped...

On one occasion when Petr Ivanovich was in the village, I was walking near their stone house. Suddenly a window was opened and I was called in. I entered and saw that my mother was there. And Petr Ivanovich said that he had already noticed everything and had made a decision that, because of my shyness and my mother's widowhood, he himself would offer to reinforce the old familial friendship by bringing our families together.

So, with a cheerful feast, we celebrated our wedding... Besides the dowry, my father-in-law, a kind man, gave me one thousand paper rubles to help my business.

(X)

According to our local customs, marriage at the age of eighteen was nothing unusual, but now it seems to me rather odd that, having been quite a shy and obedient boy in my childhood, I suddenly felt

---

[99] Eight thousand metric tons, or 16,368,000 pounds.

in myself a change in the opposite direction, as if I had obtained some particular right. Whether it was because I had got my hands on a thousand rubles, or because I felt secure in having such a father-in-law on my side, or just because when a person gets married he becomes independent and able to stand on his own feet, I found myself in a completely different situation. Various ideas arose in my head. They came one after the other. Every day I had new plans. In my imagination I projected a pleasant and smooth future, as though everything would depend solely on my own intentions. In a word, I decided to achieve for myself, at any cost, the standing that my grandfather and father had enjoyed. Their personal examples stood firmly in my head. They served as the starting point for the development of my natural ambition, which hovered over me like a whip and drove me forward.

In truth, it was no big deal for me to expand my business. I had only favorable conditions on my side. The experience I had gained in the past gave me sufficient knowledge about commodities. I knew very well when and where the best commodities were available. While trading, I made it a rule to obtain the lowest profit just to get people's confidence in order to win them as regular customers.

While expanding my commercial activities, and at the same time remaining modest, I gained confidence. If there was a shortage of cash when I was making a purchase, dealers would ask for a downpayment of half, with the rest to be paid later without interest. Confidence in me grew to such an extent that finally, when we were negotiating a deal, they did not even mention a cash downpayment. I always kept my promises, maintained the correct weights and measures, and was fair in all calculations.

My successful trading continued until 1820. My cash capital, however, grew only a little, by a few hundred rubles, because I carried out some renovations on the house and made additional purchases of some household items. Initially, my mother criticized me. She believed that I had enlarged my business beyond my capacities. She was also angry with me because she felt that I had larger household expenses than in the past, especially when I invited to dinner important people that I needed. Of course, my mother's reproaches were not pleasant but I refrained from arguing with her and continued to manage my business as I saw fit.

In the meantime, the husband of one of the female heirs of the deceased landlord, a military general, A., and his wife, came to the village. They were greeted and treated properly. They summoned the villagers and said:

"We, fellows, need to be more meticulous in the future. We need to discuss something. For example, from the entire village we collect only twenty thousand in rent a year. The deceased lord, the father of my wife, gave you privileges for many years, and we too, since his death, have continued to indulge you for the last two years. We expected you to be appreciative and yourselves raise the rent you pay, in keeping with contemporary costs. We don't want to talk about the past—let it pass—but you should understand our kindness and try to value us for it in the future."

The bailiff and the household elders replied with bows that they were very grateful for everything and prayed to God for the landlord's health and honored the memory of his deceased father. The landlord responded to this, smiling:

"Well, this is no bad thing. Thank you for remembering the late landlord. But do not forget that now we need money. We do not want to increase the rent, but instead we will do this: collect two hundred thousand rubles right now, pay it in advance, and we will not require anything from you for the next ten years. Since you are all well-off people, it will not be difficult to fulfill our request. Well, what do you say to that?"

In this way, the lord addressed a completely unexpected question to the village meeting.

Everyone was taken aback and could hardly speak a word. Having misunderstood their silence as agreement, the landlord continued:

"So you will do as I have said? Will you?"

Again there was no response.

The lord then continued:

"Well, men, be careful to pay everything exactly."

"No, father. We cannot!"

These words suddenly came out of my mouth. And at this very

moment replies started to pour out from other places, as though from a sack. One said: "No, our benefactor, it is no joke to gather two hundred thousand! Where would we get it from?" "We are so 'well off' that we ourselves are often in a need of a ruble," another bawled.

"But look what houses you have built for yourselves," smiled the landlord.

Here people began to speak out:

"So what, houses! What are houses to us? To us they are our bread. We are not agriculturalists. Our land is only 1,130 *desiatinas*[100] for 1,300 souls. We support ourselves by trade and commerce alone. We pay our rent with no arrears. What else do you want?"

The noise got louder.

Having met such a decisive refusal, the landlord, thinking perhaps "What's the point of my talking to these fools," looked at us, smiled again, turned away, took his wife's hand, ordered the bailiff to prepare the carriage and bring the horses, and left at once for Yaroslavl'.

We began to feel relieved, but our happiness did not last long. The heirs, after obtaining from the civic chamber (*grazhdanskaia palata*) a confirmation that such and such an estate of theirs was not encumbered, mortgaged the entire estate of 1,300 serfs to the Council of Trustees for twenty-five years and received two hundred fifty rubles per soul, which totaled 325,000 rubles. Two months later, the landlord's order was read out clearly at a village gathering called for the purpose.

"Because of the twenty-five-year loan of 325,000 rubles from the Council of Trustees, plus interest, thirty thousand rubles per year are required. The estate administration is duly obliged to collect this sum annually from the peasants in addition to the annual rent of twenty thousand. The total annual dues of fifty thousand will be redistributed by specially appointed people at their discretion, so that no household shall fail to pay its share. Otherwise, under the

[100] 3,051 acres.

bailiff's charge, those who fail to pay are subjected to the following: young people to immediate military conscription; those unfit for military service to work in the Siberian metallurgical mills."

(XI)

In the midst of wordless silence, interrupted by deep gasps, they finished reading the ghastly order... At that very moment, for the first time in my life, I tasted the sorrow of my status as a serf. At that very moment, for the first time, a grievous question arose in my naive mind: "What are we?" My heart was breaking into pieces and urging me to speak out, but looking around at the sorrowful faces, and hearing only solitary whispers, I managed to hold back my passions and keep them inside me.

The events shocked not only me: such a huge obligation was of extraordinary concern to everybody. Indeed, this obligation seemed to us unlawful. But what could one do? In those days peasants were prohibited from complaining against their landlords. Willfully refusing to pay the lord would mean stamping ourselves with the stigma of rebellion; if we attempted stubborn arguments we would be subjected to harsh punishment, which would reduce everyone to complete impoverishment. The gathering ended with the writing of a formal verdict on ourselves: payment of the requested sum according to the received order, laying our hopes on God. No one wanted to deprive himself of the village of his birth: it was better to deny ourselves a holiday treat just to avoid trouble. The only consolation was our unrestrained freedom to engage in economic activities.

Despite the common hardship, our family, thanks to the Most High, did not sink into complete poverty. My business endeavors proceeded well. We had no shortage of food. I always paid regularly the dues, about two hundred paper rubles, levied on me. But I thought constantly: "Why did our landlord do this to us?" I began to pay attention to what, up until this moment, had never occupied my thoughts— the local peasant way of life.

10.
Reading lesson

LIFE OUTSIDE THE VILLAGE OBSERVED

(XII)

In spite of everything, it turned out that our situation was not too bad. We had a neighbor, Ivan Ivanovich, who lived not far away from our village. He was a first-rate debauchee and was fond of urban beauties. He lived permanently in his village; endlessly, and without count, he took money from his peasants. Whatever he demanded had to be brought at once, otherwise a whipping would follow.

In this way a landlord, who was by no means young, robbed his peasants and beat them with or without reason until they finally rebelled and threatened him... Ivan Ivanovich realized that things were bad and decided to get along with his men peacefully. He bought them two kegs of vodka and pledged that, in the future, he would never again mistreat them. The people were satisfied with that. Because Ivan Ivanovich was an incorrigible ladies' man, he flirted with one local young lady from a modest family. The family realized that it might be good for them to entice and capture this goose. They seemed to pay no attention to his pranks until a certain moment when they finally caught the fellow and forced him to marry. But because he had run up so many debts in his youth that he could barely repay, his finances were in a terrible state. Since he could no longer get anything from his peasants, on the advice of his father-in-law he borrowed a large amount of money (I don't know how much) from the Council of Trustees, having mortgaged twelve hundred souls.

All hell broke loose. Visit after visit—the new couple wanted to live in the city no less—evenings, carriages, equipment: everything required money. The household finances, however, remained as they had been. In five years they repaid the loan interest, but afterwards the entire debt was placed on the shoulders of the peasants, as happened in our case, too. Only they did not have the trade and the commerce that we had.

This person was not evil but just a sort of spoilt child, careless, and a poor manager. Our other neighbor, Lev Petrovich, was of a different type. He came from an old noble family and owned 300 souls and many wood lots. In his youth he had been in state service somewhere and had achieved the title of provincial secretary. He hung around the notables and skillfully cheated them at cards. By such tricks he gained himself a nice amount of bonds and securities in the savings bank. He married and moved to the countryside. His unhappy wife, exhausted by his cruel treatment, died after three years. She left him a son, Leonid L'vovich, who even in his childhood did not get on well with his father and moved to the city to live with his aunt. Later, this son found a bride in the city and married.

After his wife's death Lev Petrovich not only drove his men out to act as beaters while hunting, but he also coerced all the young female peasants to come to perform night duties at his house, one after the other. For disobedience he punished them with a birch rod or put an iron collar on their neck for an entire month.

Eventually the peasants could take no more, and through his huntsmen they informed the landlord that they would no longer tolerate his misdeeds and, if he continued his misconduct, they would make short work of him their own way.

Initially Lev Petrovich was angry and wanted to have them all flogged, but he then changed his mind because he had no one at hand to protect him. He was afraid that he would bring trouble on himself, as had happened in Pereiaslavl' district, where the peasants, under cover of darkness, went for the landlord and his wife and left them for dead. He put an end to the night duties. He got married for a second time to a non-noble woman, since no nobleman would allow his daughter to marry him, despite all his money. No noble lady would be attracted to him, with his swarthy face and his habit of repeating a favorite saying: "Oh, business is business, earth is earth, everyone is Christian."

So for money, and with the help of his flunkies, he got married to a young woman from the petite bourgeoisie. He took this poor little thing to his estate house and boarded her up in a narrow wing. The unlucky woman languished there for fifteen years, giving her tormentor two sons.

Meanwhile, Lev Petrovich, having been stymied with respect to night duties, began to plague his peasants on economic matters. His arable lands were not very large and the peasants had no problem ploughing them. But he wore them out with other burdens: cutting firewood in the forest and transporting it twenty *versts*[101] to the city; extorting money and flax; and requiring each peasant woman to spin a certain amount of yarn during the winter and, in the summer, to weave and dye a certain quantity of linen cloth, gather a certain quantity of mushrooms, and pick a certain quantity of cherries. Each family was supposed to bring a number of eggs and a quantity of butter. Furthermore, no marriage could take place without Lev Petrovich's permission, for which he took a special fee in money, flax, and home-made cloth. He was such a master of his affairs that, when he noticed that his peasants had had successful crops, he kept it in mind. Then, after they had sold their produce, he would appropriate the income from all of them, one at a time, under the pretext of "saving the money." He would tell them, "You are a fool, you will squander everything on drink, but I will save it for you." The peasant would hesitate, claiming that he needed to buy a horse or something else for the household, but Lev Petrovich would say, "You will waste your money, you rascal. When you need a horse, I will give you one." Or he would simply say, "You blockhead, do you want the birch rod?"

So, in a word, the peasants reached the point where they no longer cared about their household economy, "Because, in any case, Lev Petrovich will find out about our earnings and take them away." He was very devious too, so that even outsiders were careful

[101] 21.3 km or 13.3 miles.

to keep away from him. From among many episodes, I recall one in particular.

He had a landless peasant, a not particularly young man. This man followed the schism.[102] He often lived as a vagrant and stayed, sometimes nearby, with one or another of his fellow-believers. He had nothing that one could take, but Lev Petrovich thought up the following trick. He filed a complaint in a local court against this peasant, Ivan Kondrat'ev, claiming that on a certain day of a certain month he had disappeared without saying a word. In fact, Lev Petrovich knew perfectly well that this peasant was either on the estate, walking back and forth from one home to another, or was visiting his fellow-believers who welcomed him as a guest. They did not see him as a runaway, since the estate where he lived was only six *versts*[103] away and they knew that he had not escaped but had just traveled back and forth between them and home. A long time passed after the landlord filed his charges. Ivan Kondrat'ev continued to walk back and forth between his village and his fellow-believers. Then, Lev Petrovich sent to the same court an appeal that "such and such a runaway peasant was hiding at such and such a place" and requested an official search.

They sent an officer, who took Ivan Kondrat'ev right from a prayer house. The evidence was clear. They arrested several other people for "harboring" him and delivered them all to the city to stand trial. Lev Petrovich demanded from the peasants two thousand rubles in compensation, but, since the court members themselves received payments from the Old Believers, after some red tape they reduced the amount to six hundred by way of compromise...

So there's your Ivan Kondrat'ev! He was remembered for a long time. Lev Petrovich only laughed, saying, "One needs to teach the peasants to become smarter." But when he came to our local marketplace, the neighboring landlords were unwilling to give Lev Petrovich so much as a bow as they passed him...

---

[102] He was an Old Believer.
[103] 6.4 km or 4 miles.

In the end, even Lev Petrovich became kinder during the year before his death. He set free his domestic servants and stopped demanding the earlier requisitions from his peasants. Even some poor peasants got things from his farmyard, some a horse, some a cow. He gave others some lumber for building and a little money.

Lev Petrovich was quite a fine fellow, but there were even better examples. One old nobleman, along with a band of spongers, moved to his countryside estate and took to hunting with hounds. One day, a peasant boy (the nobleman had three thousand souls there) accidentally hit a hound from the landlord's kennels in the leg with a stone. When he saw that his Nalet was limping, the landlord became incensed and asked, "Who injured the dog?"

The kennel attendants had to reveal the boy's identity. They produced the boy. He confessed.

In the morning, the landlord ordered preparations for the hunt in full complement. They went to the field and took their places near the forest, the hounds were let out, and the borzois were held on leads. There they brought the boy. The landlord ordered that the boy be stripped of his clothes and set loose in the field to run. Then they let out the dogs from all the packs to chase him—literally to hunt him.[104]

The borzois approached the boy, sniffed at him, but did not touch him... His mother got there in time; she had run through the forest. She clasped her child in her arms. They dragged her back to the village and again set the dogs loose. The mother went insane and died within three days.

It was said that when Emperor Aleksandr Pavlovich[105] learned

---

[104] Fyodor Dostoevsky apparently describes this incident in his *Brothers Karamazov*. In a conversation with his younger brother Aleksei, Ivan Karamazov refers to a similar episode, of which he had learned from a journal. See *The Brothers Karamazov* by Fyodor Dostoevsky, trans. Andrew R. MacAndrew (New York: Bantam Books, 1981), 292, or F. M. Dostoevskii, *Brat'ia Karamazovy* (Petrozavodsk: Karel'skoe knizhnoe izd., 1970), 266.

[105] Alexander I (r. 1801–1825). On the reign of Alexander I see Alan Palmer, *Alexander I, Tsar of War and Peace* (New York: Harper and Row, 1974).

about this incident he ordered the landlord to be put on trial. But the latter, when he heard that news of the affair had reached the tsar, committed suicide.

I also remember two brothers, A* and I* B.[106] They were not locals, but many rumors circulate in our country. The news about them reached us, too.

These two brothers, T–skie nobles, were the founders of the Sh* works in 1755, which subsequently became famous and encompassed vast resources.[107] The works earned enormous profits. Of the two brothers, I* was especially capable and industrious, but extremely mercenary. He was a past master at appropriating other people's property without caring much about how he did it. He armed all his people and was a sort of leader. He always traveled with a group of twelve staunch fellows and gave out orders like a bandit. The initial setting up of the works required a lot of land and forests, which belonged to the Kasimov Tartars, who would not agree to sell the lands. So, I* took it upon himself to cut down and set fire the trees, and wound up killing many people. And the neighboring landlords, whose lands I* needed and desired, suffered a great deal at his hands as well. He would make a deal and offer a generous price, complete the transaction, invite the person to his place to receive the payment, pay everything in full, and then treat everyone with great generosity. But in the evening, as the drunk and overfed guests made their way back home, I* would send his special lackeys to murder them and take the money back. I* would then give his men a generous reward for this service. Nobody dared to resist I* or expose him. There was no way to bring him to justice in the local courts. He even arranged special protec-

---

[106] Purlevskii probably meant the Tula entrepreneurs, brothers Andrei and Ivan Batashov, the sons of a wealthy Tula metallurgy entrepreneur Rodion Batashov. The family initially belonged to the peasant and petit bourgeois social estates, but later Andrei and Ivan obtained noble titles. Between 1755 and 1783, the two brothers possessed about eleven metal mills. *Metallurgicheskie zavody*, 1: 225.

[107] Here Purlevskii refers to the Shepelevskie works, which belonged to Ivan Batashov. See note 108.

tion in the Imperial Senate, when his affairs became known there. In the factory management office there should still be a letter from Senator L., who urged I. B., "Van'ka, your affairs stink, you should stop. Otherwise you will get into serious trouble and we, too, will fall into disgrace."

But I* did not stop. Proof of his savageness emerged—human skeletons were found in the walls when they tore down the old mill building.

However, I will say this: all these examples are exceptions. Among the nobles there were many intelligent individuals, practical and deserving of respect. And people from other social estates also did evil things. Here is an example. It comes from the very Sh* works I spoke of.

In 1783 the whole estate was divided between the brothers B. Ivan gained four plants,[108] one hundred and fifty thousand *desiatinas* of land, including about one hundred and ten thousand *desiatinas* of forest, eighteen thousand peasant souls, nine thousand of whom worked in the plants, and an industry valued at one million two hundred thousand rubles of circulating capital and two thousand rubles of net profit. After his death all this passed to his only daughter, who married General D. D. Sh.[109] The general initially took good care of the estate's economy but soon got bored with such a demanding task. Under his control the financial situation worsened, and they eventually needed a loan of eight hundred thousand rubles from the Council of Trustees. Almost all this amount they spent on building an enormous theater near the plants and on supporting a group of foreign actors. The management of the plants was exclusively in the hands of serfs. There was no proper landlord's control and direction but only stupid strictness. On the surface, production at the works was maintained in proper order, but

---

[108] These were the Vyksunskii, Veletminskii, Doschatyi and Unzhenskii plants. After 1783 Ivan founded several more plants. After his death, the Ivan Batashov enterprise passed to the Shepelev family through the marriage of Ivan's only daughter to D. D. Shepelev. After that, the enterprise was known as the Shepelev Works. *Metallurgicheskie zavody*, 1: 225.

[109] D. D. Shepelev.

in reality there were various kinds of fraud and plundering going on. After the death of the general, his two sons, Ivan and Nikolai, educated and titled gentlemen, inherited the property. But they, too, paid little attention to the estate's affairs. The youngest, Nikolai, did not even want to be personally involved in the estate management and handed it over to his brother and brother-in-law. Their activities in connection with the plants were limited merely to signing various official papers without any proper attention.

Just at that moment a certain man appeared on the scene. In a tavern near the main works a townsman from Elabuga, by the name of C., had served as a barman for many years. He made himself popular with the mill workers by acting as a fence for commodities stolen by them. In this way he made a fortune for himself. Once he and the plant manager, a serf, made an agreement to deceive the mill owners. That year there had been a poor grain harvest. The price of rye flour approached one silver ruble a *pud*, while, in contrast, the price of iron fell. In cahoots with the plant manager, C. cooked up a contract and slipped it among other papers waiting for the owner's signature. The contract gave C. the right to supply grain for three years, fifty thousand *pud*s [110]of grain a year in exchange for iron of any kind that C. needed, at an equal *pud* per *pud* rate. During the first year the plant did not lose very much, but in the two following years, when good grain harvests lowered the price to twenty-five kopecks a *pud* and the price of iron rose, the plant lost almost ninety kopecks per *pud*.

Having noticed the error, the mill owners attempted to withdraw from the contract, but C., following a formal court decision, forced the plant to fulfill it. An investigation disclosed the manager's violations and, after a whipping, he was exiled to Siberia, but the contract remained in force. Other underhanded affairs were also carried on by C., but this did not prevent him from becoming rich and, with the powerful backing of Z., an influential man of that time, from receiving medals, and eventually the Order of Empress Anna, to hang round his neck.

[110] 50,000 *pud*s equals 800,000 kg.

Still, God's judgment awaited him and he was punished. As he was on his way to his patron to receive the Order, blood began to pour from his nose and he died within the hour. His unlawful wealth was gradually dispersed and his family lived in Moscow in virtual poverty.

I can tell you more about these plants: as time went by, things got worse and worse. The debts grew to such an extent that the operation could get no credit at all and they only managed with great difficulty to continue to pay off the loan from the Council of Trustees. The matter ended as follows: the richest part of the estate, with woods and mines for the plant's production and with mills in central Russia near Moscow and the Nizhnii Novgorod fair and with excellent water transportation, declared itself bankrupt in 1846, after which everything came under the management of the Council of Trustees.

(XIII)

These examples illustrate the affairs of nobles and peasants. But are there no bad merchants, who pick on nobles and shout at peasants?

I will retell a story about one former Muscovite celebrity, the wool manufacturer P. M. A. His wool production was of irreproachable quality and brought him quite a nice profit. But his greed and self-interest could not be satisfied by honest labor. He decided to gain even more wealth and, out of the blue, declared himself bankrupt.

He got away with it. Nor was it too difficult to do. For the deal he made was not entirely unprofitable for his lenders, and they all hoped that his business would bring them returns in the future. But A. already had in mind another trick. Having tasted the success of his first experiment, and with the help of two accomplices, he started to keep double accounts. In one book he listed the real transactions and in the second he recorded bogus losses. He did this insidiously for ten years, during which time he nonetheless managed to secure another loan for his business. After making a nice profit from the loan, A. sent out circular letters to all his creditors inviting them to visit him one evening. Although they had no knowledge of what was going on, they foresaw something unpleasant, as a consequence of which those who lived in Moscow came to him in person. When the visitors saw that two assistants of A. (his very accomplices) were greeting them and that the manufacturer appeared only after everyone had gathered, they realized that something nasty was going to happen. Pretending to be ill, and under the guise of emotional stress, he started his performance by making a bow, then, with false humility and meekness, spelled out the fact that, due to the difficulties of his situation, he was unable to repay his debts, which reached two million. In order to prove this statement he presented his accounting books, which showed a deficit of one million...

This caused some commotion among the creditors, who took a look at the books, turned over the pages, went back and forth across the room, thought the matter over this way and that, and reached an agreement to reschedule the debt payment for four years.

Well, things moved on, but when the first payment was due he paid nothing. They again considered the issue and agreed that, since A. could indeed not repay in full, they would let him pay fifty kopecks per ruble within a year. One unfortunate creditor was so dismayed by this shameless plundering that, on his way home, he jumped from the Kamennyi Bridge into the river and drowned himself.

To our scoundrel this was water off a duck's back. He did not even fulfill the new terms. Using ruses and tricks he compelled his creditors to take his enterprise under wardship. He managed to worm himself into the main factory administration. The debits were repaid by profits from the factory. But in the end A. repaid scarcely anything and the million remained in his pocket.

Well, there is nothing more to say. He fooled people with his cunning. But could he deceive God? God's judgment suddenly struck A. in the form of a painful disease. For seven years he looked more dead than alive; no medical treatment could help. For three years he could eat nothing but a spoonful of broth. He sought help from the monasteries, and even enriched one with large donations, but finally died amid terrible suffering. After his death his million went in part to his accomplices and in part to his distant relatives, because he had never married and had no family.

Yet there is another case I can recall regarding the merchant way of life. There were two brothers, wealthy, hearty, and hospitable persons, all of which did them credit. Their hospitality, however, was not limited to keeping their house open to people but involved a passion for the noble way of life. This applied not only to themselves, but, after their lavish dinners, they displayed antique possessions about which they understood nothing. Furthermore, one of the brothers decided to impress people with a greenhouse, which cost him fifty thousand. The other built a house near his factory for one hundred thousand rubles, not for permanent residence, but just for occasional visits. And their mama made equal efforts. She had built, at her own expense, a huge five-domed church, also for a hundred thousand rubles in silver. So they wasted money endlessly and, when their business got into trouble, left their creditors with nothing.

There is also the case of a first guild merchant in Moscow, P. I. Kzh., who traded with tea on a large scale. His activities were carried out in Kiakhta[111] through his assistants, while here he traded with tea wholesale, not trusting anybody but himself to sell even one single *tsibik*[112]. He was so mistrustful and tightfisted that he even went himself to the marketplace every day to buy provisions for the family, expenses which, on weekdays, amounted to no more than one paper ruble. The cooking and all the other housework was done by one single female cook. On holidays his wife made pirogi herself and obediently carried out all her husband's orders. He seemed satisfied only when he could save a penny on the tiniest thing. He was an incredible niggard! His assistants from Kiakhta returned to Moscow each April with personal reports. In these

---

[111] The Kiakhta commodities exchange was an important commercial site between Russia and China.

[112] A tea chest which weighs between 40 and 80 Russian pounds (one Russian pound being 409.5 grams).

reports they would never state the real expenses, on pain of being fired by the merchant. They had to be cunning and round all the numbers down in order to make the appearance of the strictest thrift in everything, otherwise even the most honest and naturally economical among them would lose his position.

Unintentionally, in order to cover up the difference between the amount they had actually spent and the amount they reported, they developed the habit of deceit. One of his assistants told me that when they returned to Moscow from Kiakhta and were staying in Moscow in order to buy goods for Kiakhta they secretly obtained funds from the salesmen, which they used afterwards to cover up the merchant's unreported expenses. They did the same in Kiakhta, too, when they exchanged goods. They retained for themselves only small amounts equal to their wages. After all, during those three months when they lived in Moscow and stayed in the merchant's house, they were supposed to lay in firewood for the entire year, clean up his courtyard and stable, mend the driveway in front of the house, and do all the dirtiest work in person. By doing this work, they were supposed to prove their zealousness in meeting the merchant's needs. Otherwise he would have fired them, saying kindly, "Well, dear, I am dismissing you because you don't want to bother yourself with hard work in my presence. Think for yourself: How can I rely on your work in my absence?"

Kzh. was stingy not because of concern for his family and heirs but only because he enjoyed opening his chest, looking at the sacks of gold coins, and re-counting his Treasury bonds. He never gave anything to the church, the needy, or any charitable institution. He never even participated in public charities. And what about his family? Even the most modest pleasures were denied them. The gates of his house were always locked in the evenings: there was neither entrance nor exit for the family or anyone else. Even his only son and heir was denied a proper education. His learning was limited to reading, writing, and counting on an abacus. When this son was seventeen, the merchant forced him to marry the daughter of his favorite assistant, V. I. Sh. His sole intention was to avoid big wedding expenses and to have a new daughter-in-law from a modest family, who would be more obedient to the existing household order... In a word, the merchant's family regarded him as an oppressor and looked forward eagerly to his death as they would a holiday.

In 1819 he died. It turned out that the merchandise and securities he had were valued at sixteen million in paper money and that he had four million rubles deposited in the Savings Bank on the condition that his direct heirs were to use only the interest and that the capital would remain for the next generation. All this passed to his only son, who, while his father was alive, was not able to touch even a single ruble. And now he had suddenly acquired millions! Even an experienced person would have felt giddy, so what hope was there for a merchant's son who had depended totally on his father and hardly even knew of the existence of the theater...

At that moment a certain Kv., also the young son of a merchant, turned up. A spoiled fellow, he had no difficulty in getting close to the none-too-clever Kzh. After a short while Kv. introduced him to a company of debauchees and gradually enticed him into dissipation. The family business was handed over to his father-in-law, the Vereisk merchant V. I. Sh., who was concerned only about his own interests and cared little about helping his son-in-law. Even he took part in the revelries. In two years Kzh. and Kv. became famous for their pranks. Once they got an archimandrite drunk and gave him a ride across the city with a pumpkin on his head instead of his *klobuk*.[113]

For this piece of mischief Kv., as the instigator, was sent into military service while Kzh. got away with a fine. Later on he became so arrogant that once, in 1824, as an honored member of the Moscow Commercial and Practical Academy, and having learned that it needed money, he had the insolence to offer it thirty-five thousand rubles on condition that the academy nominate him to a Vladimir of the Fourth Degree or Anna of the Third.[114] This did not work out, of course, and he cut his donation down to two hundred rubles.

Nevertheless, his silly ambition did him some good. Deeply offended by the refusal, this rich man wished to get an award at any

[113] The headdress of an Orthodox priest.
[114] Here Purlevskii is referring to the Order of Vladimir of the Fourth Degree and the Order of Empress Anna of the Third Degree.

cost. He set up a model wool factory, of a sort that no reasonable owner would ever have built. C. bought a plot of land in the countryside, seven *versts* from Moscow, erected factory buildings and living apartments there in gothic style, and secretly ordered from England steam engines and factory equipment. At the time this was no easy thing to do because machine imports from England were prohibited and Kzh. got them only for a huge amount of money. After a while the factory began to operate and produced woolen cloth of the best quality. For this Kzh. became well known and finally got the Vladimir Order for the public good he had done.

But Kzh. had no luck. Helped by the tariffs in those days he might have returned a profit, but he took no personal interest in the business. He turned over the factory's management to a careless and mercenary person. Consequently, in 1830 he lost ten million rubles at one stroke. His enthusiasm for the factory waned. On Kzh.'s appeal the government allowed him to withdraw the four million from the Savings Bank in order to continue to support factory production. But because of his carelessness and drunkenness even this money did not last long. Subsequently he began to take loans at high interest, and finally the factory went into bankruptcy. After numerous sequestrations the factory literally fell into ruin. They got only thirty thousand for it, just enough for repaying outstanding debts, although its original cost had been more than three million. The owner found himself in a very unpleasant situation.

This was sad, because it was at his enthusiastic initiative that Moscow factories began to produce woolen cloth for the Chinese market, as a consequence of which it was no longer necessary to order from abroad woolen cloth of the so-called Miziritskii brand for the Kiakhta fair. Also, Russia began to manufacture other types of woolen cloth needed for internal consumption, particularly after the introduction of the shpanskii breed of sheep and after foreign machinery imports became easier and cheaper (80 percent cheaper than those bought by Kzh.).

I have become so absorbed in my stories that I have jumped from the twenties to the thirties and forties, and have got bogged down in the realm of notorious merchants. Now let me get back to my former life under serfdom.

11.
Peasant women's head dress

12.
Peasant women's autumn dress

THE BITTERNESS OF SERFDOM REALIZED

(XIV)

I have already mentioned that, from my childhood, I had a great love of reading. But before my marriage I mostly limited my reading to books of ecclesiastical content and read very few secular publications. After I got married, I began to read real literature. And my curiosity was aroused to such an extent that I could spend entire nights sitting with my books. The poetry of those days particularly attracted me. As a result, I still retain in my memory many compositions and entire plays by certain poets. The intelligent judgments of talented writers always won out over my simple-minded peasant views and the superstitions usual for a commoner. Reading exposed my ignorance about almost everything.

Nevertheless, this somehow lowered my self-esteem. Although I agreed with the ideas I read about and although my mind could comprehend them and my traditional assumptions were gradually vanishing, their place was being taken by some confusing and diffuse thoughts, which I not only barely understood, but which also aroused in me a skepticism about what I was reading. Of course, the cause of all this confusion was my own non-systematic reading.

Perhaps this was for the better, because I was cautious about reaching hasty agreement with those brave ideas, which could hardly be applied to the actualities of my serf condition. After all, I was not a single man. I needed to think about and take care of my family...

Although it scarcely satisfied my spiritual objectives, my business provided support for the household. Thus I decided to continue my life according to the familiar path of commerce. Later on, the books gradually took over, and the life I led also encouraged this outcome. Previously, before I burdened my mind with thoughts about my serf status, my life objectives were limited to achieving a status similar to that of prominent, well-off fellow-villagers, or at least a status that would do no injury to the memory of my father and grandfather. But after the event when the landlord forcibly increased our obligations, his power over us and the humiliating, slave-like condition of all society made me uneasy all my life.

How to get rid of this centuries-old entrapment and free my family from it as well? I had to think over many things, while the hair turned white on my head... What could a married man, with limited knowledge, without money, and without connections and protection, do, and, more importantly, what could a serf do...? In truth, my feelings of irritation and my dissatisfaction could easily have got me into serious trouble. More than anything else, the temptation that I experienced as regards people who made huge fortunes through dishonest tricks made me unhappy. But the Almighty God preserved the purity of my credo. It was not in my nature to accept shabbiness, and my mind recognized only fair ways of making money. I had to make all my deeds accord with this belief.

The limited commercial activity I pursued held out no promise of sufficient funds in the future to buy freedom. Therefore I decided to expand my trade. Having closely examined and considered all the possible ways of doing business with which I was familiar and handy, I decided on local commodities, purchased in large quantities for the port of Archangelsk. I had the fortunate idea of calculating the balance of price increases as the commodities passed through several hands.

The result, in my view, was quite encouraging. Consequently, I dared to report my calculations to Arkhangelsk, to the trading company of Brant, with which I was completely unfamiliar. Of course, I gave a careful account of every detail, according to the circumstances and realities. I offered to become the house's local commercial agent. But could I hope for success? I presented them with no support for my credentials, not even a simple letter of recommendation!

Nevertheless, I suddenly received a letter from Wilhelm Ivanovich Brant with a clear order to purchase flax. (It was, I remember, one morning in 1822.) After that, in the next mail, I received thirty thousand rubles... Before I had a chance to turn around, he sent me sugar from his plant on commission...

This business continued until 1830. Only once during those eight years did I happen to visit Arkhangelsk and meet my boss in person. Usually, the annual balances and reports were carried out via mail. It is hard to believe, but this is the truth. In my life this event became an encouragement for me and for new undertakings, which were no less profitable and significant. The year following Brant's offer I decided to contact the manager of the Alexandrovsk Imperial Plant, General Aleksander Iakovlevich Simpson...

And the result? He, too, gladly agreed to entrust me with the purchase of flax. I engaged in this activity for the next several years. Meanwhile, my local business continued as it had been before. The St. Petersburg flood of 1824 damaged my goods and brought losses of seven thousand rubles. Nonetheless, in 1826 I had fifteen thousand of my own in circulation. With such a sum of money one could buy one's way out of serfdom, a state that always seemed to belittle me in the eyes of free people.

But, as time passed, this cherished idea weakened... Whether because serfdom did not restrain the freedom of my commerce and my access to loans, or because I could not withdraw from my business activities the money necessary for buying my freedom, I can hardly say now. I only know that I delayed again and again until 1826, when an event occurred before my very eyes that made me feel all too sharply my bitterness of my lot as a serf.

(XV)

I have already described how the surrounding villages belonged to our estate and how in the past, beginning with the first owner who came after Repnin, the alcohol tax farmer, the peasants were sent to work in the manorial factory. On the second division of the estate, twenty-three villages with a cotton factory—in total about one thousand six hundred souls on the census register—passed to our landlord's nephew, who in 1818 sold all his property to a prince by the name of *. Later on, although still serfs, these peasants were quite prosperous.

But thirty or forty years before that things were different. At that time, the peasants were administered by a hired German manager who kept them downtrodden in every way. Besides labor duties, he also resorted to moral violence against them. Even marriages, in the form of voluntary unions, as had actually been the case, gradually disappeared, and almost every marriage was concluded by order of the factory administration. For these occasions they set a time, once a year, when, according to a special list, they called grooms and brides to the administration office. There, under the personal direction of the German manager, they formed couples, which afterwards, under the supervision of the administration, were sent directly to the church where a priest blessed several weddings at a time. Peasants' priorities and desires were of no concern.

In this sorrowful state of affairs, accompanied by constant complaining among them, a few peasants sent written complaints directly to the landlord. But the latter, unfortunately, paid no attention to them. Instead, he relied fully on the manager and, giving no consideration to their complaints, asked the manager to "teach" all the complainers the "domestic" way.

And the fun began: every day a severe flogging. The peasants' endurance was finally exhausted. In 1828 almost all the village, without being called on, gathered by the factory office in order to question this infidel: Why such tyranny? Having seen the big crowd, the sly German realized what was up. If he had just talked to the people and showed them the landlords' order, the indignation would have ended.

But no. He made his servants tell the people that he would talk with them in the evening. Then, that evening, he again delayed talking to them until the next morning, saying that he was sick, and he gave the people a glass of wine[115] and bread for dinner. On the

---

[115] Purlevskii probably referred to vodka, which in Russia is also sometimes called "wine" or "white wine."

following night, however, without saying a word, he rushed to the provincial town thirty *versts*[116] away and appeared before the governor with the charge that the prince's peasants were disobedient and were in a state of rebellion, as though he himself had barely saved his life by fleeing. In the meantime, the peasants were not even thinking of rebellion and, sincere as they were, did not have the least suspicion of trickery. They accepted the manager's kind response, a glass of vodka and bread, as signs of special favor and hope for the future. They headed for their homes peacefully and, in the morning, following what the manager had told them, again gathered around the factory business office, where they fully expected to achieve a fair resolution.

No such thing! All at once several troikas carrying representatives of the authorities, military troops, and the manager pulled up. The casual way in which the crowd had gathered could scarcely have proved the manager's slander, but he had apparently bribed someone. The representatives of the authorities shouted, "Why have you dragged yourselves here, mutineers? Go home, or every tenth man of you will receive a flogging."

The peasants were so shocked by this unexpected turn of events that they did not dare explain what the real story was but simply stared without saying a word. The authorities ordered the troops to seize from the crowd all those who were lingering, put them in chains, and take them to the city as the instigators. They also filed a report, formally signed by the authorities, that the mutiny had been pacified. But not only did the clerk refuse to sign the report, he also filed a protest stating that the people who had gathered had not been allowed to explain the reason for their meeting and that, in fact, at the first demand they had obediently left for their homes. However, his appeal was not shown to the governor and the arrested peasants were brought to trial. Nevertheless, the district court immediately released the arrested as innocent.

Everything seemed to have happened for the better, but then turned out for the worse. Although the accusations of rebellion

---

[116] 32 km or 20 miles.

were withdrawn from the peasants, their complaints against the manager were ignored and everything remained as it had been. Out of malice following his defeat, the manager began to take revenge and oppress the peasants even more harshly, reporting to the landlord that the peasants were rebellious and that the district court had indulged them in their rebellious ways. The landlord again avoided the issue. Mistrusting and ignoring the court decision, he instead used his own legal powers as a landlord. He ordered that all the discharged peasants, without further consideration, be sent either into military service or to live in Siberia. The peasants, meanwhile, had never believed in a happy ending and had a presentiment of the trouble coming from their oppressors. They wrote an appeal to the Highest Name, in which they described everything in detail, and all the literate people from all the estate villages signed it. As the landlord's strict instruction reached the factory office and rumors about it spread, the peasants immediately sent four selected people to St. Petersburg to seek the tsar's protection. This delegation presented an appeal to Emperor Nikolai Pavlovich[117] in person and received from the Minister of the Interior a document allowing their free return to their native village.

In the meantime, while the delegation was traveling, the estate authorities began to take peasants from the villages, according to the landlord's direction. Waiting for the return of the delegation, the peasants decisively refused to give up their fellow-countrymen, doomed to perish. They stated that if the lord wished, they would only go into the military or to Siberia all together or no one would go at all... On the landlord's behalf the manager appealed to the governor. The governor sent troops to all the villages and reported an insurrection to the minister.

A terrifying commotion had begun. A whole garrison occupied the villages, terrifying the peasant households. Then, I remember, in June, they brought the inhabitants from all the surrounding villages to the village closest to ours and detained them. I myself was a wit-

---

[117] Nicholas I (r. 1825-1855). On his reign see Bruce W. Lincoln, *In the Vanguard of Reform: Russia's Enlightened Bureaucrats, 1825-1861* (DeKalb: Northern Illinois University Press, 1982.)

ness of this. The people were placed around, and in the middle stood the authorities. About one hundred people, the younger ones, were given a sound whipping. Everyone, having crossed themselves, endured the punishment without saying a word. Those who were stronger tried to protect the weak ones and stepped forward. Women cried sorrowfully, children screamed. I am barely able to retell what I saw... The representatives of the authorities themselves turned away their faces and lowered their eyes.

But it must be that guiltless suffering does not vanish without leaving a trace. That day was the last day of peasant suffering, out of which a new order emerged. In a short while the German manager was replaced by a new one, a Russian, an indulgent and kind man, who found ways to replace labor duties with machines and work contracts. Some peasants began to pay money rent and others worked at the factory voluntarily, for money which was counted against their labor duties. After a few years the situation improved. Many peasants even became prosperous.

It is worth mentioning that, after a while, some importunate supplicant, a Finn, shot the prince with a gun at his house in St. Petersburg, in the presence of his family. Was this not God's Judgment on the prince for the torturing of his peasants, and were not the latter in their turn suffering for the sins of their predecessors? We cannot be judges of this.

(XVI)

Before this sad event I had viewed my serf status more or less with indifference, but the impression of what I saw that day revived my old desire to free myself and my family from bondage, even at the price of all the cash I had. I occupied myself with this desire for two years: I used various means, brought presents for certain people I needed and for the landlord's closest servants, yet received only a little hope. Finally even this little vanished, due to zealous but not very subtle solicitations made by my kind friends, who overpraised me in the hope of helping my efforts. In particular, my commercial acquaintances made solicitations for me.

Then one of them informed me that the landlord would not hear of losing me, because he "intends to employ you for business of his own."

As a matter of fact, shortly after this the estate management received instructions to "inform such and such a peasant of our estate and oblige him, under his signature, and with the strict responsibility of the management, not to dare bother in future with solicitations for his redemption. Moreover, well-known people are soliciting for him, probably with the goal of using him for their own commercial affairs. Therefore, keep special note of him until our further directions."

With a heavy heart I listened to the landlord's instructions and signed a statement that I would not bother him in the future...

13.
Peasant-migrant and a merchant

MY ACTIVITIES IN ESTATE LIFE

(XVII)

Until 1828, while paying my rent regularly, I participated but little in the communal affairs of the village that did not touch me directly. I spent all my time on my commercial pursuits. I frequently heard complaints from my fellow-villagers about the bailiff's abuses of power. Since I was a relative of his and got on well with him, I told him many times informally to improve the way he carried out his duties. I would tell him this in a straightforward, friendly way. This offended him, and he began to treat me unfairly. Either he would delay the issuing of a travel document for me, on the pretext that the landlord needed me there, or he would persecute me with anything else he could think up. As regards travel passes, there was no great problem.[118] Paying no attention to the bailiff's whims, I went directly to the landlord, who never hindered my commercial activities and always gave the order to issue me with a travel pass. On some occasions he reprimanded the bailiff in no [uncertain terms].

Once, instead of a travel pass, I unexpectedly received an order to be ready for a sale of iron produced at the landlord's mills at the Nizhegorod fair...[119]! The rumors about the lord's counting on me had come true.

[118] In order to leave the estate temporarily, serfs (just as any social estate, including the nobility) had to have a document (internal passport, pass, or permit) which they obtained from the local authorities (bailiffs of landlords). Gorshkov, "Serfs on the Move," 633–39.

[119] On the Nizhegorod fair see Anne Lincoln Fitzpatrick, *The Great Fair: Nizhnii Novgorod, 1840-90* (New York: St. Martin's Press, 1990).

The honor of being entrusted to conduct this business was very unwelcome to me. Not because I feared the business but because I was concerned about our stupid rules of trade. They constrained commerce as if it, too, were in serfdom, or as if customers had to buy our mill's products and therefore must absolutely comply with the instructions given to those who were sent to the fair. Much about these instructions can be seen from the following.

For example, they prescribed: 1) Iron, of all types must be sold at a price higher, not cheaper, than the prices of all other producers, such and such a type for such and such a price. You are responsible for any neglect. 2) Purchases must be paid for in cash. No amount should be sold before payment. 3) All quantities sent to the fair must be sold without fail, and thereafter a certain amount of money should be sent by mail to the Siberian mills, a certain amount transferred via the bank to us in St. Petersburg, and a certain amount retained until new instructions. 4) If, contrary to expectations, products cannot be sold at the set prices, report to us and wait for our instructions about price reductions...

Can business be carried out in this way? And who, from the free estates, would agree to undertake such a responsibility, when in wholesale it is not customary to require the customer to pay the full price before delivery? Rather, one always relies on an advance payment, a memo, or just a verbal promise... My situation was quite risky; but what could one do about it? Argue with the landlord?

On the first occasion I received under my supervision about one and a half hundred thousand *puds*[120] of iron. Although a significant quantity, I had no difficulty in selling it. Right from the time of its opening in 1817, I was quite familiar with the Nizhegorod fair and its commercial rules. It was not difficult to meet with the chief iron dealers. Not hindering myself by strictly observing the owners' petty restrictions I acted freely, according to the general situation of business at the fair. Consequently, with God's help, I completed my

---

[120] 2,400,000 kg.

first sale quite successfully and received the landlord's appreciation and a reward of five hundred rubles.

This had such a positive effect on my self-esteem that I nearly gave up my idea of redeeming myself from serfdom.

(XVIII)

Around this time our communal management became more and more chaotic. The peasants' complaints about the bailiff annoyed the landlords to such a degree that they finally ordered the estate management office to appoint me as a bailiff. I was to take charge of all forthcoming communal affairs and to ask the former bailiff for detailed reports about all previous activities in village life.

Although this prestigious assignment certainly flattered my self-esteem, it hardly made me happy. Indeed it scared me, because I had no experience in village governance. In light of my objective view of this matter, I repeatedly implored the landlords to spare me from the new responsibility they had imposed on me. They disagreed and kindly confirmed my appointment. They suggested that I find a responsible, knowledgeable assistant so that I could continue my own commercial activity without hindrance.

This solution allayed my concerns and allowed me to undertake the new tasks in addition to my existing ones. I began to dig into communal matters. When I studied the commune's outstanding affairs, various abuses came to the surface. They were so serious that the former bailiff even voluntarily returned some of the communal money he had spent. To my misfortune, under cover of submissiveness to his lot he became very hostile toward me, which I noticed but to which I hardly paid any attention. For my part, I tried to finish the initial inspection in a quite lenient, routine way, without spreading gossip or initiating any scandals.

Having finished with the outstanding business, I moved on to establish my own routine. Although I had become a public person without any desire on my part, I still faced the task of dealing with communal needs in a fair way. For instance, I was one of the first to notice that our important commercial village did not even have a school. Nobody had ever taken care of this.

I immediately told the commune that we needed a school and it enthusiastically supported my opinion. I drew up a plan. Of course, the landlords' agreement was needed. They did not put up any objections, and indeed commissioned me to take care of all educational matters.

Everything was approved! The archpriest of our church became the theology teacher. The local authorities sent someone to teach grammar, calculus, and orthography... By the day of the grand opening, seventy boys who wished to study had come forward. During the first year this number increased to one hundred. In the exams, in the presence of the principal, many pupils did excellently. In general, all were able to read and write, whereas in my childhood a boy, even a gifted one, having spent the same amount of time with a priest, could merely mumble the syllables of the Psalter. Even then he would mostly rely on memory, as I had experienced myself.

Because I found this success so rewarding, I decided to suggest a trade school in addition to our regular school. This was necessary in Velikoe because we never engaged in agriculture but for generations had dealt in trade and commerce. Unfortunately, this idea met with no success. The landlords refused to donate five thousand rubles in cash, and the village communal assembly denied approval and even openly resisted my plan, regarding it as a king of corvée...

Then I noticed that the area of our residence, which already had three thousand souls of both sexes, did not have any local medical facility. The ill could benefit from only occasional visits by a district physician, and even these were only for the prosperous and in exceptional cases. Everyone else either perished without medical care or resorted to the drugs of a quack. I was very upset at this situation. However, I did not dare to suggest my idea to the village commune, because I knew about their deeply rooted superstitions. Instead, I presented the idea directly to the landlords.

They approved it immediately and, in addition, themselves arranged for the arrival of a physician in private practice by the name of Mikhail Loginovich. They set the doctor's salary, which they agreed to fund, and made arrangements for an appropriate living place, servants, and firewood. This good man rendered us great service, or one might even say kindness. He set up a small village pharmacy and taught several boys pharmaceutics and nursing arts—all this, thanks to the landlords, without the slightest burden to the commune. The commune, after a while, realized the usefulness of what had been done and appreciated our doctor, who also valued the simple openness of our peasants. I was very pleased by this mutual respect. Mikhail Loginovich was always an esteemed guest in my house.

Finally, the idea of improving our cottage industries and village crafts occurred to me. All commerce and trade were to be carried out on the basis of absolute honesty. In truth, one needs to have patience to make commerce fair; but in return, when your reputation for fairness has reinforced your business reputation, everyone will gladly do business with you and even allow your trade to predominate with them. Besides honesty, trade must not confine itself to old-fashioned production methods but must follow the needs of the times. Profit should come not from the use of cheap, low-quality or counterfeit materials for the manufacturing of goods, but from skillful mastery and the durability of the products.

Now I need to reiterate what I have already said in part. From time immemorial, in my birthplace, Velikoe, women had been highly skilled in producing fine linen cloth, which was famous everywhere for its quality. This women's labor was fully rewarded until foreign technical innovations developed cheaper and improved modes of production. In the face of competition, our women should have taken advantage of their previous profits to develop new methods. But instead of doing everything they could to readjust their work to the new conditions, they tried to serve their own interests by adding cotton threads in the weft. At first they earned huge profits from doing this, because even a skilled dealer was unable to notice the fraud.

But, of course, the admixture became apparent when the product was put into use. We began to lose our reputation for fine linen cloth, to such an extent that people stopped buying it! Therefore, I made a plan and suggested to the commune that it forbid this evil fraud. At first no one seemed to understand me; they could not see where their real advantage lay. I took my concerns to the village's chief management. Not only did they pay no attention to the issue, they returned my papers to me with a reprimand and prohibited me from bothering them in the future with "ideas of this kind that can disrupt the collection of rent... "

14.
Peasant-migrants carpenters

MY FUTURE FATE RESOLVED

(XIX)

This was how my plans on village governance developed. In general, everything was fine and everyone was satisfied with me. I also occupied myself with selling iron products at the Nizhegorod fair. Until 1830 this part of my activity also went well. As a result, I always received praise and rewards. In 1830 we sold our iron at prices even higher than we had expected.

Unfortunately for me, an outbreak of cholera killed two of my assistants, who had taken care of transporting iron products from the Siberian mills and delivering them, according to my sale orders, to the customers, as we had always done. On one occasion it turned out that the load arrived short by one thousand two hundred *puds*[121], which, according to contemporary prices, amounted to 4,560 paper rubles.

I was not responsible for matters concerning the formal acceptance and delivery of goods. However, the office of the general estate management required an explanation from me. Soon afterwards they sent an inspector to Velikoe. Having examined the estate's business, and having talked to the friends of the deceased transportation assistants about the lost iron, the inspector could find nothing obvious or even anything questionable to hold against me. Even so, correspondence on this matter continued for an entire year... Obviously there were no complaints against me on the part of the landlords, since they would not have stood on ceremony in

---

[121] 19,200 kg.

their dealings with me. The chief estate manager, with the former bailiff (whom I had replaced) at his side, were at work here. Still, it was clear that I could easily influence the manager in my favor, as suggested by his obvious attempts at extortion in his letters. Frankly, considering my case to be just, I unfortunately did not want to stoop to corrupt patronage. I was even happy in the thought that the current scandal would bring an end to this burdensome assignment of mine.

In 1831 my desires were realized, but not as I had expected. A manager of the Siberian mills was assigned to go to the fair for the purpose of selling iron. Meanwhile, I was ordered to go to St. Petersburg to explain things in person...

This turn of affairs promised nothing good. Another inconvenience was the fact that, in the meantime, my own business required personal attention and direction. However, I had to obey and, after putting the estate management in order and passing everything to my assistant in November, I arrived in Petersburg at the beginning of December.

I immediately appeared before the manager of the estate main office. I was greeted by him in a kindly enough way, since I was personally acquainted with him. However, he was very reserved and vaguely promised to report to the landlords (who were in the office once a week) about my arrival. I was allowed, by the way, to occupy a room in the lord's house. Two weeks passed and I had still not been summoned.

Without waiting to be called I decided to report to the landlord, General A., himself. I had always enjoyed his favor and had no difficulty in arranging the meeting. His valet, a fellow-villager, immediately reported to the general about my visit and I was invited to go to his study. There, my future fate was settled, so I will relate our conversation in detail...

EPILOGUE[122]

Unfortunately, with these very words, the original manuscript comes to an abrupt end. The autobiographer's death in 1868 prevented him from finishing the story of his life. His further fate is known only from oral histories, told to me by people well acquainted with him. I will retell it in brief. I am sorry for the lack of details, which would perhaps be of great interest.

The serf bailiff, Savva Dmitrievich Purlevskii, who fell into disgrace as the result of another's guilt and because of hostile slander, came out of his lord's study neither dead nor alive. The scene had been terrible. The landlord strictly ordered him to "go back to the village immediately and wait there for further instruction."

This terrifying phrase "wait for further instruction" overwhelmed Purlevskii. He imagined the kind of reprisals that he himself had been witness to many times—corporal punishment, maybe the "red hat," perhaps even Siberia... Usually logical, on this occasion he lost his head completely and immediately decided to flee. Where to? There was no need to think much about this: where the Old Believers, who probably often fled his village, usually ran to—beyond the Prut, beyond the Danube!

On that very day he disappeared from St. Petersburg. The realization that his sudden disappearance would serve as proof of his guilt made him uneasy. In order to discourage the landlords from thinking of him as a runaway and of his flight as a confession of

---

[122] The following text was written by the journal editor Shcherban.

guilt and escape from deserved punishment, on his way he sent a letter to the landlords in which he explained in detail that he could not be even technically at fault in a matter that had occurred on its own, without his physical presence. He explained the moral motives that had caused him immediately to look for escape, abandoning everything, because of the possible consequences of the slander against him.

When he had left home for St. Petersburg, Purlevskii had taken with him only a small amount of money, and after his expenses in St. Petersburg and the fare for the trip back, he arrived in Moscow with only fifty rubles, twenty rubles of which, that he had put in a wallet, were stolen... Using what was left he somehow got to Kiev, where he had not so much as a kopeck. He, a prosperous peasant, homeowner, and bailiff, had to go on foot to Kishinev.

The Prut was a stone's throw from there, but he had no money to arrange a convenient, safe passage, which was usually provided by the frontier Jews for a decent sum of money. There was nothing he could do. Alone as he was, our poor industrious fellow approached the river in the dead of night, cut some cane, tied it into a bundle, lay on it, pushed off with his legs, and struck out down the river.

The current took him to Moldova. After a few days our fellow found himself in Iassakh, exhausted, ragged, hungry, and without money. There he encountered quite a few Russians who had fled, in particular Skoptsy[123], who were making a living mainly in the carrier's trade. Purlevskii joined them. They sheltered their fellow-countryman, gave him food, and took him into their service. The former homeowner became a servant, and was glad of it.

Nevertheless, he soon began to make his way up: his honesty and hard work were noted. He was entrusted with a carriage and began to work as a carrier, and received a salary calculated upon a share of his receipts. He started to make money and became prosperous, and even began to dream about buying his own carriage

---

[123] A Christian religious sect in Russia. The members of this sect practised celibacy, self-castration and eschatology. The Skoptsy receive attention in Laura Engelstein, *Castration and the Heavenly Kingdom: A Russian Folktale* (Ithaca: Cornell University Press, 1999.)

sometime in the near future. But once, while half asleep, he over-heard a conversation: "He is a good fellow, we need to convert him to our faith..."

Staunchly Orthodox, Purlevskii had never particularly admired the Old Believers from his own village and he certainly could not imagine himself as a convert to the Skoptsy! Because he had heard that the Skoptsy often used force he became very scared, and at the very first opportunity he fled beyond the Danube to the fisheries, where he joined the Nekrasovtsy.[124]

He lived there for two years, receiving much kindness and enjoy-ing many things. One thing distressed him: he missed his country, his village, and his family, of whom, in spite of the letters he sent, he received no news. He could barely keep himself from returning. But how? He was still a runaway serf!

The Nekrasovtsy were very curious about what was going on in Russia and subscribed to newspapers. Once, in around 1834, they read in *Odesskii vestnik* that, at the representation of Count Vo-rontsov and by a Merciful Decree from on High, all runaway serfs who had not committed crimes were allowed to settle freely in the Novorossiisk area, where they would be welcomed.

Having gathered all his few savings, Purlevskii immediately went to Odessa and obtained the status of a townsman. There he found employment as a waiter in a bar. The owner admired Purlevskii and he became a manager.

A certain magistrate's officer used to go to that bar. He was very fond of Savva Dmitrievich and in a short while this acquaintance-ship proved quite useful. Someone in Odessa sent a denunciation that such and such a runaway serf from Velikoe was living there. The estate management was almost ready to drag him back, but the magistrate's officer and the Kherson criminal chamber defended his registration in the estate of Odessa townspeople.

---

[124] An Old Believer group who settled in the Kuban' region in the early eighteenth century. For more information on the Nekrasovtsy see *The Modern Encyclopedia of Russian and Soviet History*, Joseph L. Wieczynski, ed. (Gulf Breeze, Fl.: Academic International Press, 1976), under Nekra-sovtsy.

At that time Iakhnenko and Simirenko established their famous sugar refinery. The above-mentioned magistrate secretary was a nephew of theirs. On his recommendation, Savva Dmitrievich was given a job as a commissioner in the newly opened business. Initially things did not go well. Once, for example, in 1847, he went to Astrakhan' with fifty kegs of sugar, lived there for three months, and did not sell a single one. He was about to return with nothing when a local dealer of colonial goods, I. I. Kozlov, came to him and bought all fifty kegs.

With the help of this dealer business went well and the position of S. D. Purlevskii was solidified. He entered the merchant estate. Prior to the 1850s, he traveled throughout all of Russia and lived mainly in Sevastopol. In 1852 he moved to Moscow, where, until his death in 1868, he remained a commissioner of the famous Iakhnenko and Smirnenko Corporation. In 1856 he bought freedom for his only son for two thousand five hundred silver rubles (his mother and wife, it seems, had died long before then). When the Manifesto for the Emancipation of the Peasants was announced, the old man, having returned from a church service, sat at the table and, without saying a word, dissolved into tears...

From such tears an endless, inexhaustible sea of appreciation flowed around the throne of the empire's Reformer!

INDEX